Dramascripts
Oliver Twist

CHARLES DICKENS

Adapted by
Guy Williams

With notes and activities by
Penny Chatwin

Nelson

Thomas Nelson & Sons Ltd
Delta Place
27 Bath Road
Cheltenham GL53 7TH
United Kingdom

ıⓉᴘ® Thomas Nelson is an International Thomson Company
ıⓉᴘ® is used under licence

Oliver Twist – the script
© Guy Williams 1969
The right of Guy Williams to be identified as author of this play has been asserted by Curtis Brown Ltd in accordance with Copyright, Design and Patents Act 1988.

Introduction, activities and explanatory notes by Penny Chatwin
© Thomas Nelson 1998

Designed and produced by Bender Richardson White
Typesetting by Malcolm Smythe
Cover illustration by Dave Grimwood
Black and white illustrations by John James
Printed in Croatia by Zrinski

This edition published by Thomas Nelson & Sons Ltd 1998
ISBN 0 - 17 - 432548 - 7
9 8 7 6 5
08 07 06 05

CONTENTS

SERIES EDITOR'S INTRODUCTION

Dramascripts is an exciting series of plays especially chosen for students in the lower and middle years of secondary school. The titles range from the best in modern writing to adaptations of classic texts such as *A Christmas Carol* and *Silas Marner*.

Dramascripts can be read or acted purely for the enjoyment and stimulation that they provide; however, each play in the series also offers all the support that pupils need in working with the text in the classroom:

- **Introduction** – this offers important background information.
- **Script** – this is clearly set out in ways that make the play easy to handle in the classroom.
- **Notes** explain references that pupils might not understand, and language points that are not obvious.
- **Activities** – at the end of scenes, acts or sections – give pupils the opportunity to explore the play more fully. Types of activity include: discussion, writing, hot-seating, improvisation, acting, freeze-framing, story-boarding and artwork.
- **Looking back at the Play** – this section has further activities for more extended work on the play as a whole with emphasis on characters, plot, themes and language.

OLIVER TWIST, the story of a workhouse orphan's flight to the dark and contaminated city of London, is the novel most closely linked with the name of Charles Dickens. First published in monthly episodes in *Bentley's Miscellany*, it was an immediate success, delighting *The Times* which printed sections of the novel as it appeared and inspiring six different stage versions within weeks of its completion. And the story retains its hold on the public imagination today through the famous cinematic adaptation of 1948 and the brilliant West End musical, *Oliver!*

Dickens began work on *Oliver Twist* in 1837 before he had completed *The Pickwick Papers*. He was an energetic young man of twenty-five at the time, already famous as a writer: he wrote swiftly with serious intent. The opening chapters of the novel were a direct and angry attack on The Poor Law of 1834 which made poverty a crime and imprisoned the hungry and homeless in grim workhouses. *Oliver Twist* is a bitter outcry against social injustice; it is also the first novel in the English language in the which a child is the central character.

Dickens slipped details of his own childhood experience into this novel just as he was to do with later ones. Oliver's helplessness in the dark, criminal world recalls the vulnerability of the writer forced into the frightening reality of factory work at the age of twelve.

Despite its serious purpose, *Oliver Twist* is full of comic life and fired by excitement and suspense. The climax of the novel occurs in the brutal murder of Nancy and the flight of her lover, Bill Sikes, pursued by a violent mob. Dickens caused a sensation when he selected this episode for reading to a large audience. It was the closest that one of his readings ever came to a theatre performance.

This condensed, script version contains all the dramatic intensity of the original with nightmarish scenes of corruption and violence, vivid characters and the authentic speech of nineteenth century criminals. It is also faithful to the angry political message of the opening workhouse scenes of the novel. Above all it brings to life the orphan, Oliver, who against all the odds retains his innocence, the child who, made reckless by hunger, dared to ask for more.

THE CHARACTERS

OLIVER TWIST, a serious and well-spoken young man looking back at his childhood.

MR LIMBKINS, Chairman of the Workhouse Board, a particularly fat, red-faced gentleman in his fifties.

OTHER MEMBERS OF THE BOARD, prosperous gentlemen.

MR SLOUT, the Master of the workhouse, an overweight middle-aged man.

MR BUMBLE, the beadle: portly, bad-tempered, self-important, middle-aged.

MRS CORNEY, the matron of the Workhouse, an ample, middle-aged widow.

YOUNG OLIVER, a pale and undernourished workhouse orphan, nine years old at the start of the play.

A TALL WORKHOUSE BOY, nine or ten years of age.

A THIN WORKHOUSE BOY

OTHER WORKHOUSE BOYS

MR SOWERBERRY, the parish undertaker, a tall, gaunt man in his forties.

MRS SOWERBERRY, his wife, a short, thin, squeezed-up, angry woman.

NOAH CLAYPOLE, a charity boy in his teens, apprenticed to Mr Sowerberry.

CHARLOTTE, a servant to Mrs Sowerberry, in her teens and fond of Noah.

JACK DAWKINS (THE ARTFUL DODGER), a young pickpocket about Oliver's age.

FAGIN, a dealer in stolen goods, very old and shrivelled.

CHARLEY BATES, another young pickpocket apprenticed to Fagin.

TWO OTHER PICKPOCKETS

BILL SIKES, a brutal house breaker, thirty five years old and stoutly built.

NANCY, a young woman, the mistress of Bill Sikes.

MONKS alias **EDWARD LEEFORD**, a pale and mysterious man of twenty six, Oliver's half-brother.

MR BROWNLOW, a kind old gentleman in his sixties.

MRS BEDWIN, his housekeeper, a motherly old lady.

MR GRIMWIG, his friend, a stout old gentleman of sixty-one.

A WORKHOUSE WOMAN

OLD SALLY, a dying woman who has lived in the workhouse for many years.

AN OLD WOMAN OF THE WORKHOUSE, attendant in the infirmary.

AN APOTHECARY'S APPRENTICE

TOBY CRACKIT, as his name suggests, a housebreaker (in his thirties).

TOM CHITLING, an eighteen year old thief.

KAGS, a broken-nosed, scar-faced robber of fifty years.

With: **MEMBERS OF THE WORKHOUSE, LONDONERS AND PRISON OFFICERS.**

OLIVER TWIST
ACT 1 ❖ SCENE 1
THE PARISH WORKHOUSE

(OLIVER enters)

OLIVER   Have you ever been hungry? So hungry that you haven't   1
been able to do anything but think about your stomach?
And how you are going to fill it? I've been like that for
weeks and months at a time. You see, I was born at a
Charity Workhouse, where my mother had been taken in
an exhausted state. She had been found lying in the street
the previous night, having walked a great distance, for her
shoes were worn to pieces. She died, poor thing, when I was
a few minutes old. I was brought up by the worthy
Members of the Board of Guardians . . .   10

*(The MEMBERS OF THE BOARD enter, with MR SLOUT, the
Master of the Workhouse. They sit down at an official table, to
one side.)*

. . . and by their Beadle, Mr Bumble . . .

The Charity Workhouse and the Board of Guardians *Since
Elizabethan times, each parish had been responsible for its own poor and
destitute. In 1834, a new Poor Law came into effect forcing any person in
need of help from the parish to live in a workhouse. New, larger workhouses
were built to serve several parishes and were under the control of a board of
governors. Life in the workhouse was made as unpleasant as possible to
discourage the poor from asking for help.*

Beadle *a parish officer responsible for making arrangements to deal with the
poor of the parish. After 1834 the beadle had to take instructions from the
Board of Governors.*

(MR BUMBLE enters, and bows to the Board.)

. . . This is Mrs Corney, the Matron of the Workhouse . . .

(MRS CORNEY enters, and curtseys to MR BUMBLE.)

. . . When I was eight or ten months old, the Members of the Board decided that I should be farmed out, and I was sent to a small Branch Workhouse some three miles off. But the time soon came when they wanted me back.

MR BUMBLE   I shall be away for a few hours, Mrs Corney, upon porochial business connected with the porochial orphans . . .

(MRS CORNEY inclines her head.)

. . . The child that was half-baptised Oliver Twist is nine year old today.

MRS CORNEY   Bless him!

MR BUMBLE   And notwithstanding an offered reward of ten pound, which was afterwards increased to twenty pound. Notwithstanding the most superlative, and, I may say, supernat'ral exertions on the part of this parish, we have never been able to discover who is his father, or what was his mother's settlement, name, or con – dition.

MRS CORNEY   *(Raising her hands in astonishment.)* How does he come to have any name at all, then?

MR BUMBLE   *(Drawing himself up with great pride.)* I inwented it.

Branch Workhouse *Oliver spent his early life on a 'baby farm' for children of poor people who lived in the workhouse – hence 'that I should be farmed out'.*

porochial *Mr Bumble's pronunciation of 'parochial', meaning relating to the parish.*

inwented & Vilkins *Bumble and a number of other 'low-life' comic characters in the writings of Dickens pronounce their 'v's as 'w's.*

20

30

MRS CORNEY	You, Mr Bumble!
MR BUMBLE	I, Mrs Corney. We names our foundlings in alphabetical order. The last was an S, – Swubble, I named him. This was a T, – Twist, I named him. The next one comes will be Unwin, and the next Vilkins. I have got names ready made to the end of the alphabet, and all the way through it again, when we come to Z.
MRS CORNEY	Why, you're quite a literary character, Sir!
MR BUMBLE	*(Evidently gratified.)* Well, well, perhaps I may be. Perhaps I may be, Mrs Corney. Oliver being now too old to remain at the Branch Workhouse, the Board 'as determined to have him back here. I am going out myself to fetch him, as the porochial delegate, the porochial stipendiary. I will see him at once.
	(MR BUMBLE picks up his porochial cane and goes out. MRS CORNEY goes to a large copper, and stirs.)
THE CHAIRMAN OF THE BOARD	The intentions of the Poor Law Acts were undoubtedly good, Gentlemen, but alas! the poor people don't seem to mind coming to our Workhouse. Unless we are very careful, our Workhouse may become a regular place of public entertainment for the poorer classes; a tavern, where there is nothing to pay; a public breakfast, dinner, tea and supper all the year round; a brick and mortar elysium, where it is all play and no work!
OTHER MEMBERS OF THE BOARD	Hear! Hear! It's disgraceful! It's a scandal!
THE CHAIRMAN	But we are the fellows to set this to rights. We'll stop it in no time. We must establish this rule: that all poor people

40

50

60

stipendiary *'person who receives a wage'*

a brick and mortar elysium *'a paradise on earth in the form of the workhouse building'* shall have an alternative. We'll compel nobody, not us. They shall have the alternative of being starved by a gradual process in the house, or by a quick one out of it. Are we agreed on that, Gentlemen? . . .

(General agreement.)

. . . Mrs Corney! . . .

(MRS CORNEY stops stirring and goes to curtsey to the Board.) 70

. . . Mrs Corney, we have contracted with the waterworks to lay on an unlimited supply of water. We have contracted with a corn factor to supply periodically certain quantities – certain small quantities – of oatmeal. We have instructed dear Mr Slout to issue three meals of thin gruel only per day. You may give the paupers one onion each, Mrs Corney, twice a week, and as a treat half a roll on Sundays. Do you understand, Mrs Corney? There's no saying how many applicants for parochial assistance may not start up in all classes of society if we don't look ahead. We must make 80 relief inseparable from the Workhouse, and from gruel. That'll frighten people.

(MR BUMBLE appears, with YOUNG OLIVER.)

YOUNG OLIVER   Are we nearly there?

MR BUMBLE   Nearly there? We're there. Now just you smarten yourself up, me boy. It's a Board night, and the Board has said that you are to appear before it forthwith . . .

They shall have the alternative of being starved by a gradual process in the house, or by a quick one out of it *Dickens uses bitter humour to show his anger at the injustice of The New Poor Law (1834).*

gruel *This is a thin porridge made by boiling oatmeal in water.*

pauper *'a destitute person; someone supported by charity.'*

forthwith *immediately.*

(He taps OLIVER with his porochial cane.)

. . . So wake yourself up . . .

(He taps OLIVER again.)   90

. . . And make yourself lively. And follow me.

(MR BUMBLE takes OLIVER before the Board.)

. . . Bow to the Board, Oliver.

OLIVER   Seeing no Board but the table, I bowed to that.

THE CHAIRMAN   What's your name, boy?

*(YOUNG OLIVER trembles. MR BUMBLE gives him another tap
behind, which makes him cry out.)*

**A MEMBER IN
THE WHITE
WAISTCOAT**   The boy's a fool.

THE CHAIRMAN   Boy, listen to me. You know you're an orphan, I suppose?

YOUNG OLIVER   What's that, Sir?   100

**THE MEMBER IN
THE WHITE
WAISTCOAT**   The boy is a fool – I thought he was.

THE CHAIRMAN   Hush! *(To YOUNG OLIVER.)* You know you've got no father
                        or mother, and that you were brought up by the parish,
                        don't you?

YOUNG OLIVER   *(Weeping.)* Yes, Sir.

**THE MEMBER IN
THE WHITE
WAISTCOAT**   What can the boy be crying for?

A THIRD MEMBER   I hope you say your prayers every night and pray for the
                        people who feed you, and take care of you, like a Christian?

YOUNG OLIVER   Yes, Sir.

THE CHAIRMAN	Well! You have come here to be educated, and taught a useful trade . . .	110
THE MEMBER IN THE WHITE WAISTCOAT	So you'll begin to pick oakum tomorrow morning at six o'clock.	
THE CHAIRMAN	Take him away, Mr Bumble . . .	

(MR BUMBLE leads YOUNG OLIVER aside.)

. . . Well Gentlemen, I think that concludes our formal business, so if you would care to join me in a glass of the parish's wine, I think we may adjourn.

(THE CHAIRMAN signals to MR SLOUT. The Master of the Workhouse pours wine for THE MEMBERS OF THE BOARD, who move off, with their glasses, to a not-far-distant place. As they do so, the PAUPER CHILDREN who have been sitting round the stage move up with their bowls and spoons towards the copper. MR SLOUT gives YOUNG OLIVER a bowl and a spoon and puts him at the very end of a bench. MRS CORNEY ladles a little gruel into each bowl.) 120

MRS CORNEY	Shall you say Grace, Mr Slout?
MR SLOUT	Silence, please, paupers. For what the Good Lord and the kind Board of Guardians have seen fit to give us to eat, let each and every one of us be thankful. You may begin . . . 130

(The PAUPERS eat ravenously, and then staring at the copper as if they would like to devour the very bricks of which it is composed.)

pick oakum *to pick old rope apart so that the fibres can be used to make the hulls of ships watertight: a tedious job, often given to convicts and the inmates of workhouses.*

a glass of the parish's wine *Dickens is suggesting that some of the parish money collected from the rates has been spent on wine for parish officers and the Board rather than to feed the desperately hungry workhouse children.*

the copper *a boiler made of copper.*

... And now, Mrs Corney, our own meals await us, I believe, in our own quarters.

(MR SLOUT and MRS CORNEY go, MRS CORNEY sniffing and observing 'smells good!' as she leaves the stage. MR BUMBLE, attendant upon the Board, is unaware of the PAUPERS. Their attention is still fixed on the empty copper.)

OLIVER   For my first six months in the Main Workhouse, this system   140
was in full operation. It was rather expensive at first, in consequence of the increase in the undertaker's bill, and the necessity of taking in the clothes of all the paupers, which fluttered loosely on our wasted, shrunken forms after a week or two's gruel. But the number of workhouse inmates got thin as well as the paupers; and the board were in ecstacies.

At last, we became wild with hunger. There was one boy among us, tall for his age . . .

(The TALL PAUPER stands up.)

. . . who hadn't been used to that sort of thing, for his   150
father had kept a small cookshop.

THE TALL PAUPER   It's not right, I tell yer. It's not right. I get's so 'ungry I would just about eat the cove sleeping next to me, these nights . . .

(There is a grim chuckle.)

. . . You can laugh! You'll laugh on the other side of your fices if you wakes up one morning and find I've 'ad your leg off. I will, too, if they don't give me another basin of gruel every day. I'll stop at nothing when I gets desperate!

For my first six months in the Main Workhouse, this system was in full operation. *Oliver means the system of making conditions in the workhouse as unattractive as possible. So harsh were the conditions that a number of workhouse inhabitants died of starvation.*

cove *a slang term meaning 'fellow'.*

A THIN PAUPER   *(Standing up.)* Tosher's right. We're all starving to death. But   160
what are we going to do about it?

THE TALL PAUPER   We'll have to ask for more, that's all.

ALL PAUPERS   For more? . . . But that's . . . But Mr Bumble . . . But . . .
But . . . But . . .

THE THIN PAUPER   That's gammon. We won't get more at all. We'll just get a
taste of old Bumble's stick for our pains. We get enough
stick-oil on our seats as it is, without goin' and askin' for it.

THE TALL PAUPER   Well, what's the alternative? Just sit here and do nothing
until we've all withered away?

A THIRD PAUPER   It's worth a try, to my way of thinking.   170

(Murmurs of assent.)

THE THIN PAUPER   But who's going to do the askin'? You goin' to do it
yourself, Tosher, since you're that keen?

THE TALL PAUPER   Me? No. We'll draw lots. That'll be fair, won't it?

(There is absolute silence.)

. . . Well, won't it? . . .

(Still silence.)

. . . Are you all afraid, or something? . . .

*(He looks at each of the PAUPERS in turn. Each, under the TALL
BOY'S surveillance, shakes his head. Last, the TALL BOY looks*   180
*at YOUNG OLIVER. There is a moment of tension before
YOUNG OLIVER, too, moves his head sideways.)*

. . . Well we're all agreed then. Give us some straws and
we'll do it now . . .

---

gammon *a slang term for 'rubbish'.*

stick-oil *The oil Mr Bumble used on his cane came off on the seat of the
boys' trousers when they were thrashed.*

(One of the boys passes some straws, from near the copper. The TALL PAUPER turns his back on the others and arranges the straws between his hands, so that the ends only protrude.)

. . . There you are . . .

(He turns.)

. . . All them straws is long but one, and I've bit that one off   190
short. The cove what gets the short one is the one what
asks for more. After supper tonight. See?

(He offers the straws round, and each of the PAUPERS takes one in turn.)

OLIVER I knew with absolute certainty as he took the straws round
that the short one was destined for me. I nearly cried out
'Why are we wasting our time like this? I'm the boy! I know
I'm the boy!'

*(THE TALL PAUPER stops before YOUNG OLIVER who takes
the end of one of the two remaining straws and pulls it.)*   200

THE TALL PAUPER It's the short one!

*(There are general cries of 'Oliver!' and 'Oliver Twist' . . . 'Oliver
Twist to ask for more!' . . . 'Oliver Twist to ask for more!' MR
BUMBLE, hearing the noise, appears and walks slowly across the
stage tapping the side of his leg with the porochial cane. The
PAUPERS freeze back silently in fear as he passes.)*

OLIVER The hours crept slowly by, but eventually that evening
arrived, and we boys took our places near the copper.

(MRS CORNEY comes in, followed by MR SLOUT.)

MRS CORNEY A lovely sirloin, Mr Slout, with mushrooms, and all the   210
trimmings. You never saw such a dish. The juices in that
beef! You're welcome to a slice if you'd care to look in after
the boys has had their supper . . .

(She goes to the copper, and distributes gruel.)

... Shall you say Grace, Mr Slout?

MR SLOUT   Silence, please, paupers. For what the Good Lord, the kind Board of Guardians and the Ratepayers of this Parish have seen fit to give us to eat, let each and every one of us be thankful. You may begin ...

(The PAUPERS gulp down their gruel. Then all look to YOUNG   220
*OLIVER. There are whispers and winks and even a nudge or two.
At last YOUNG OLIVER stands up and walks slowly towards the
copper. MR SLOUT and MRS CORNEY, still talking beef, are
thus rudely interrupted.)*

YOUNG OLIVER   Please, Sir ...

MR SLOUT   Yes?

YOUNG OLIVER   Please, Sir, I want some more.

*(MR SLOUT gazes in stupefied astonishment on the small rebel
for some seconds, and then clings for support to the copper.)*

MR SLOUT   *(In a faint voice.)* What's that?   230

YOUNG OLIVER   Please, Sir, I ... WANT ... SOME ... MORE.

MRS CORNEY   *(With a loud scream.)* Oh, the limb of Satan!

MR SLOUT   Fetch the Beadle! Get Mr Bumble! Get Mr Bumble! Oh, you ungrateful young devil!

*(He grabs MRS CORNEY'S ladle, and starts to belabour YOUNG
OLIVER with it. MRS CORNEY hastens to MR BUMBLE.)*

MRS CORNEY   Mr Bumble! Mr Bumble! Oliver Twist has asked for more!

MR BUMBLE   For more? That, Mrs Corney, sounds like revolution ...

a lovely sirloin *There is a cruel contrast between the succulent beef and the boys' thin porridge (gruel).*

belabour *'beat'*

(THE BEADLE needs no urging to deal with YOUNG OLIVER. Seeing that the boy has been safely pinioned by MR SLOUT, he hastens to tell the MEMBERS OF THE BOARD.)   240

. . . Mr Limbkins! I beg your pardon, Sir! Oliver Twist has asked for more!

THE CHAIRMAN   For more?

MR BUMBLE   For more, Sir. For more.

THE CHAIRMAN   Gentlemen, there appears to be a crisis in the affairs of our Workhouse. Shall we adjourn to our Board? . . .

(The GUARDIANS mount to the table at which they sat before.)

. . . Now compose yourself, Bumble, and answer me distinctly. Do I understand that Oliver Twist asked for more   250 after he had eaten the supper allotted by the dietary?

MR BUMBLE   He did, Sir.

THE MEMBER IN THE WHITE WAISTCOAT   That boy will be hung. I know that boy will be hung.

(An animated discussion takes places, in which the words 'Beat him!' 'Starve him!' and 'Transportation' are clearly heard, followed by 'Saving of expenditure!' 'Look well in the accounts!'

and 'Have a printed report published!' At last THE CHAIRMAN stands up.)

THE CHAIRMAN We are agreed, then gentlemen. The decision of the Board, Mr Bumble, is this: you shall take that ungrateful boy away   260 instantly and confine him in a dark solitary room . . .

(MRS CORNEY grips YOUNG OLIVER.)

. . . having flogged him well first, of course, on the way . . .

(Mr Bumble brandishes the porochial cane.)

. . . We shall be taking some steps to see that he is no longer a charge on our parish . . .

(ONE OF THE BOARD is laboriously inscribing the words OLIVER TWIST on a large notice.)

. . . In the meantime, you had better keep the brute on half rations . . .   270

(YOUNG OLIVER whimpers.)

. . . and give him the stick in the dining room occasionally as a warning and example to the other . . .

(A cry.)

. . . Mr Slout!

(YOUNG OLIVER is marched out by MRS CORNEY, MR BUMBLE following in full porochial majesty. THE CHAIRMAN hands MR SLOUT the notice. MR SLOUT shuffles away and hangs it up in a prominent position. One by one THE MEMBERS OF THE BOARD go across to inspect the notice, and to nod at it   280

dietary *This was the allowance of food laid down by the person in charge of the workhouse.*

Transportation! *being sent to work in Australia for life, a punishment usually reserved for convicts.*

with satisfaction, before they go out. The last is THE MEMBER IN THE WHITE WAISTCOAT.)

THE MEMBER IN THE WHITE WAISTCOAT

(Reading.) 'Five Pounds Reward. The above sum will be paid to any man or woman who wants an apprentice for any trade, business or calling, who will take a boy called Oliver Twist off the hands of the parish.' I never was more convinced of anything in my life, than I am that that boy will come to be hung.

(The first strokes of the porochial cane can be heard off-stage as MR SLOUT, left alone at the Board, raises and drains dry each of the bottles of the parish's wine before he carries them back to the Workhouse pantry.)

290

IMPROVISATION: In this scene, the Board of Guardians holds an emergency meeting to decide how to respond to the shocking behaviour of Young Oliver. In the course of the meeting, they call out *'Beat him!'*, *'Starve him!'* and *'Transportation!'*.

Working in a group of four or five, improvise their whole discussion, including phrases from the text such as those given above.

WRITING: This scene has a dramatic ending but it is also very informative. Oliver and the Chairman of the Board speak to us directly about the workhouse system and we learn other details indirectly from what is reported or done in the scene.

In a pair, list all the details about The Poor Law and the workhouse system that you can find in this scene. For example:

The Workhouse
controlled by Board of Guardians.

WRITING: Imagine that you are a young man or woman employed by the charity commissioners in 1835. You have been asked to visit a typical Parish Workhouse and to write a clear account of conditions. Describe the conditions you find and the punishment you witness in Oliver's workhouse.

ACT 1 ❖ SCENE 2
AT MR SOWERBERRY'S

OLIVER   I was taken, after a lot of bargaining, by the Parish   1
undertaker, Mr Sowerberry. It was arranged that I should go
to him 'upon liking' – a phrase which means, in the case of
a parish apprentice, that if the master find, upon a short
trial, that he can get enough work out of a boy without
putting too much food into him, he shall have him for a
term of years, to do what he likes with.

MR SOWERBERRY   *(Who is working on a coffin.)* And why not? I pay a good deal
towards the poor's rates, don't I? Haven't I the right to get
as much out of them as I can? There's not much to be   10
made, in this game. Three or four inches over one's
calculation makes a great hole in one's profits: especially
when one has a family to provide for.

*(There is a loud rap on the door, and MR BUMBLE appears in
full ceremonial outdoor rig. Behind him cowers YOUNG
OLIVER, in a clean shirt. YOUNG OLIVER is carrying all his
worldly belongings in a brown paper parcel half a foot square by
three inches deep.)*

MR SOWERBERRY   *(Without looking round.)* Aha! Is that you, Bumble?

MR BUMBLE   No one else, Mr Sowerberry.   20

MR SOWERBERRY   I have taken the measure of the two women that died last
night, Mr Bumble.

---

poor's rates *Charges paid by the better-off households in a parish to support the poor.*

full ceremonial outdoor rig *His beadle's uniform consisted of a cocked hat, a brass-buttoned coat and a staff of office.*

MR BUMBLE	You'll make your fortune, Mr Sowerberry . . .
	(MR BUMBLE thrusts his thumb and forefinger into MR SOWERBERRY'S snuffbox, which resembles a miniature coffin.)
	. . . I say you'll make your fortune, Mr Sowerberry.
MR SOWERBERRY	Think so? The prices allowed by the Board are very small, Mr Bumble.
MR BUMBLE	So are the coffins, Mr Sowerberry.
	(MR BUMBLE allows himself as near an approach to a laugh as 30 *a great official ought to indulge in.)*
MR SOWERBERRY	Well, well, Mr Bumble, there's no denying that since the new system of feeding has come in, the coffins are narrower and more shallow than they used to be, but we must have some profit, Mr Bumble. Well seasoned timber is an expensive article, Sir, and all the iron handles come, by canal, from Birmingham.
MR BUMBLE	Well, well, every trade has its drawbacks. A fair profit is, of course, allowable.
MR SOWERBERRY	Of course, of course. And if I don't get a profit upon this or 40 that particular article, why, I make it up in the long run, you see – he! he! he!
MR BUMBLE	Just so. Haw! Haw! Here! I've brought the boy.
	(At a signal, YOUNG OLIVER makes a bow.)
MR SOWERBERRY	*(Raising a lantern above his head to get a better view of YOUNG OLIVER.)* Oh, that's the boy, is it? . . .
	(He calls through to a little room behind the shop.)

snuffbox *A small container of powdered tobacco which was taken by inhaling through the nose.*

... Mrs Sowerberry, will you have the goodness to come here a moment, my dear? ...

(MRS SOWERBERRY emerges. She is a short, thin, squeezed up woman, with a vixenish countenance.)   50

... My dear, this is the boy from the workhouse that I told you of.

(YOUNG OLIVER bows again.)

MRS SOWERBERRY   Dear me! He's very small.

MR BUMBLE   Why, he is rather small ...

(He looks at YOUNG OLIVER as if it is the boy's fault that he is no bigger.)

... He is small. There's no denying it. But he'll grow, Mrs Sowerberry – he'll grow.   60

MRS SOWERBERRY   Ah, I dare say he will – on our victuals and our drink. I see no saving in parish children, not I; for they always cost more to keep than they're worth. However, men always think they know best. We'll have to do what we can with you, little bag of bones ...

(She calls her maid servant.)

Here, Charlotte, give this boy some of the cold bits that were put by for Trip. The dog hasn't come home since the morning, so he may go without 'em. I dare say the boy isn't too dainty to eat 'em – are you, boy?   70

MR SOWERBERRY   Perhaps you would care to step into the parlour and have a little drop of somethink before you go, Mr Bumble? You've had a very long walk.

vixenish *'bad-tempered'*

victuals *'food'*

dainty *'fussy'*

Somethink *non-standard spelling suggests Mr Sowerberry's pronunciation.*

MR BUMBLE	Well, perhaps, just a little drop, Mr Sowerberry, and thank you kindly.
	(CHARLOTTE puts a basin marked 'DOG' on the ground in front of YOUNG OLIVER as the adults go out.)
MRS SOWERBERRY	*(Turning back.)* Your bed's under the counter, boy. You don't mind sleeping among the coffins, I suppose? But it doesn't much matter whether you do or don't, for you can't sleep anywhere else.
OLIVER	The shop was close and hot. The atmosphere seemed tainted with the smell of coffins. I was alone, with no friends to care for, and no friends to care for me . . .
	(The light fades slowly as OLIVER is saying this.)
	. . . I wished as I crept into my narrow bed that it were my coffin, and that I could be laid in a calm and lasting sleep in the churchyard ground, with the tall grass waving gently over my head and the sound of the old deep bell to soothe me in my slumber.
	I was awakened, in the morning, by a loud kicking at the outside of the shop door . . .
	(Daylight. YOUNG OLIVER struggles into his shirt. The kicking is repeated in an angry and impetuous manner about twenty-five times.)
NOAH CLAYPOLE	*(Outside.)* Open the door, will yer?
YOUNG OLIVER	I will, directly, Sir.
NOAH CLAYPOLE	*(Through the key-hole.)* I supposed yer the new boy, ain't yer?
YOUNG OLIVER	Yes, Sir.

80

90

yer & winder *Noah's regional accent suggests his low social status.*

17

NOAH CLAYPOLE	How old are yer?	100
YOUNG OLIVER	Ten, Sir.	
NOAH CLAYPOLE	Then I'll whop yer when I get in. You just see if I don't, that's all, my work'us brat!	

(He whistles, until YOUNG OLIVER manages to open the door.)

YOUNG OLIVER	I beg your pardon, Sir. Did you knock?
NOAH CLAYPOLE	I kicked.
YOUNG OLIVER	Do you want a coffin, Sir?
NOAH CLAYPOLE	You'll want a coffin before long, if you tries to be funny with me. Yer don't know who I am, I suppose, Work'us?
YOUNG OLIVER	No, Sir.

110

NOAH CLAYPOLE I'm Mister Noah Claypole and you're under me. Take down the shutters, yer idle young ruffian . . .

(He kicks YOUNG OLIVER.)

. . . and carry them through to the yard. That's yer first job. I'll find plenty more for yer afterwards . . .

(YOUNG OLIVER tries to remove the shutters. They are too heavy for him, and there is a tinkle of falling glass.)

. . . Cor! You've broken the winder! You'll catch it when Mrs Sowerberry gits hold on yer! 'Ere, I'll give yer a hand . . .

(Together the boys struggle out with the shutters. As they return, **120** *CHARLOTTE appears.)*

CHARLOTTE	Come through to the fire, Noah. I've saved a nice little bit of bacon for you from Master's breakfast. Oliver, I've put some bits out for you on the cover of the bread-pan. There's your tea there, too. Take it away to your box . . .
NOAH CLAYPOLE	To yer kennel.
CHARLOTTE	And drink it there, and make haste, for they'll want you to

	mind the shop. D'ye hear?	
NOAH CLAYPOLE	D'ye hear, Work'us?	
CHARLOTTE	Lor, Noah! What a rum creature you are! Why don't you let the boy alone?	130
NOAH CLAYPOLE	Let him alone! Why, everybody lets him alone enough, for the matter of that. Neither his father nor his mother will ever interfere with him. All his relations let him have his own way pretty well. Eh, Charlotte? He! he! he!	
CHARLOTTE	Oh, you queer soul! . . .	

(*She bursts into a hearty laugh, in which she is joined by NOAH CLAYPOLE; after which they both look scornfully at poor YOUNG OLIVER as he sits shivering on the box in the coldest corner of the room, eating the stale pieces that have been specially reserved for him.*) 140

. . . Come on, Noah.

(*As they go out, MR SOWERBERRY can be heard offstage, singing 'The Strife is o'er, the battle won . . .' quite cheerfully. He enters, and puts on his woodworking apron.*)

MR SOWERBERRY (*Kindly.*) Good morning, Oliver . . .

(*YOUNG OLIVER stands up.*)

. . . No, sit down and get on with your breakfast, lad. I'll get the shop tidy, then I'll be ready to go out if any business has – h'm – materialised during the night. It's a nice sickly season, just at this time. To use a commercial phrase, Oliver, coffins is looking up. 150

(*MRS SOWERBERRY sweeps in.*)

rum '*odd*'

The strife is o'er, the battle won *This is the first line of a well-known Easter and funeral hymn.*

MRS SOWERBERRY   Ain't you finished your breakfast yet, bag o'bones? Hurry up. We want the basin for Trip.

MR SOWERBERRY   My dear –

MRS SOWERBERRY   *(Sharply.)* Well?

MR SOWERBERRY   Nothing, my dear, nothing.

MRS SOWERBERRY   Ugh, you brute!

MR SOWERBERRY   *(Humbly.)* Not at all, by dear. I thought you didn't want   160
to hear, my dear. I was only going to say . . .

MRS SOWERBERRY   Oh, don't tell me what you were going to say. I am nobody; don't consult me, pray. I don't want to intrude upon your secrets.

(She gives an hysterical laugh, which threatens violent consequences.)

MR SOWERBERRY   But, my dear, I want to ask your advice.

MRS SOWERBERRY   No, no, don't ask mine. Ask somebody else's.

(Another hysterical laugh, which frightens MR SOWERBERRY very much.)   170

MR SOWERBERRY   It's only about young Twist, my dear. A very good looking boy, that, by dear.

MRS SOWERBERRY   He need be, for he eats enough.

MR SOWERBERRY   There's an expression of melancholy in his face, my dear, which is very interesting. He would make a delightful mute, my love . . .

(MRS SOWERBERRY looks at him in wonderment.)

 mute *'a silent funeral attendant'*

... I don't mean a regular mute to attend grown-up people, my dear, but only for children's practice. It would be very new to have a mute in proportion, my dear. You may depend upon it, it would have a superb effect.   180

MRS SOWERBERRY   What an obvious suggestion! Why ever didn't you think of it before?

(THE SOWERBERRY'S dress YOUNG OLIVER in mourning clothes, with a black hat band that reaches down to his knees. When they have finished, MRS SOWERBERRY calls NOAH CLAYPOLE and CHARLOTTE to admire the results. CHARLOTTE is delighted. NOAH CLAYPOLE is jealous of the attention that is being showered on YOUNG OLIVER, and glowers at the new boy. There is a muffled knock.   190
MR SOWERBERRY goes to the door and speaks to someone on the threshold.)

MR SOWERBERRY   Who? Bayton? Dead? Good! . . . Yes, I'll be along at once . . .

(He speaks to MRS SOWERBERRY.)

. . . Business, dear. Sent medicine in a blacking bottle yesterday. Wouldn't take it. Gone this morning. Doesn't that show? . . .

(To NOAH CLAYPOLE.)

. . . Noah, look after the shop. The sooner this job is done,   200
the better.

(He gathers a tape measure and other requisites of his profession, and hurries out.)

MRS SOWERBERRY   The sooner our jobs are done the better, too. Dishes, Charlotte, and beds!

(THE WOMEN leave YOUNG OLIVER and NOAH CLAYPOLE alone on the stage.)

NOAH CLAYPOLE   D'you know what you are, Work'us? You're a sneak. That's

21

what you are, a work'us sneak. Promotin' yer to mute, indeed, before yer've bin in the gime five minutes. I'll pull yer 'air, I will, if yer gives me 'arf a chance. 210

OLIVER In the course of the next few weeks, I acquired a great deal of experience, both of funerals and of Noah Claypole's malevolence and jealousy.

NOAH CLAYPOLE You'll be strung up one day, and I shan't 'arf 'ave a lot of fun watching yer struggle.

OLIVER Until the day arrived when I could stand Noah's taunts no longer. The crisis came when he attempted to be more facetious still, and in this attempt did what many small wits, with far greater reputations than Noah, sometimes do 220 to this day when they want to be funny. He got rather personal.

NOAH CLAYPOLE Work'us! 'Ow's your mother?

YOUNG OLIVER She's dead! Don't you say anything about her to me!

NOAH CLAYPOLE What did she die of, Work'us?

YOUNG OLIVER Of a broken heart, some of our old nurses told me. I think I know what it must be to die of that!

NOAH CLAYPOLE Tol de rol de lairy, Work'us, what's set you a snivelling now?

YOUNG OLIVER Not you. Don't think it.

NOAH CLAYPOLE Oh, not me, eh? 230

YOUNG OLIVER No, not you. There; that's enough. Don't say anything more to me about her; you'd better not!

NOAH CLAYPOLE Better not! Well! Better not! Work'us, don't be impudent.

---

malevolence *'ill will' The delight he took in Oliver's misfortunes.*

Tol de rol de lairy *A meaningless snippet from a folk song chorus that is designed to be mocking.*

Your mother, too! She was a nice one, she was. Oh, Lor! Yer know, Work'us, It can't be 'elped now, and I'm sure we must all pity yer very much, but yer must know – yer mother was a regular right-down bad 'un.

YOUNG OLIVER   What did you say?

NOAH CLAYPOLE   A regular right-down bad 'un, Work'us. And it's a great deal better, Work'us, that she died when she did, or else she'd   240
have been hard labouring in Bridewell, or transported, or 'ung; which is more likely than either, isn't it? . . .

(Crimson with fury, YOUNG OLIVER seizes NOAH CLAYPOLE by the throat; shakes him until his teeth chatter; and throws him to the ground.)

. . . He'll murder me! Charlotte! Missis! Here's the new boy a-murdering of me! Help! Help! Oliver's gone mad! Char – lotte!

(NOAH CLAYPOLE'S shouts are responded to by a loud scream from CHARLOTTE, and a louder one from MRS SOWERBERRY.)   250

CHARLOTTE   *(Rushing in and seizing YOUNG OLIVER.)* Oh, you little wretch! Oh, you little un-grate-ful, mur-der-rous, hor-rid villain!

MRS SOWERBERRY   *(Rushing in as soon as it is safe to do so.)* Villain! Wretch! Murderer!

(CHARLOTTE, MRS SOWERBERRY and NOAH CLAYPOLE scratch and pummel YOUNG OLIVER until they are all wearied out and can tear and beat no longer. Then they drag him, struggling and shouting, but nothing daunted, into the dust cellar and there lock him up.)   260

Bridewell *a London prison, notorious for its harsh conditions.*

MRS SOWERBERRY   *(Sinking into a chair and bursting into tears.)* Oh! Ooooh! Ooooh!

CHARLOTTE   Bless her, she's going off! A glass of water, Noah dear. Make haste!

MRS SOWERBERRY   Oh! Charlotte, what a mercy we have not all been murdered in our beds!

CHARLOTTE   Ah! Mercy indeed, ma'am. I only hope this'll teach master not to have any more of these dreadful creatures, that are born to be murderers and robbers from their very cradle. Poor Noah! He was all but killed, ma'am, when I come in.   270

MRS SOWERBERRY   What's to be done? Your master's not at home; there's not a man in the house, and he'll kick that door down in ten minutes.

CHARLOTTE   Dear, dear! I don't know, ma'am . . . unless we send for the police-officers.

NOAH CLAYPOLE   Or the millingtary.

MRS SOWERBERRY   No! No! Run to Mr Bumble, Noah, and tell him to come here directly, and not to lose a minute; never mind your cap! Make haste!

*(NOAH CLAYPOLE runs out, and pauses not once for breath   280
until he reaches the Workhouse gate.)*

OLIVER   By the time Noah arrived back with Mr Bumble, the position of affairs had not at all improved. Mr Sowerberry had not yet returned, and I was continuing to kick with undiminished vigour at the cellar door . . .

(MR BUMBLE walks in, followed by NOAH CLAYPOLE.

---

she's going off *Mrs Sowerberry is having a fit of hysterics (uncontrollable weeping).*

millingtary *Noah's pronunciation of* military *(the army).*

MRS SOWERBERRY and CHARLOTTE rush to the Beadle, and gesticulate wildly.)

. . . The accounts of my ferocity, as related by Mrs Sowerberry and Charlotte, were of so startling a nature that Mr Bumble judged it prudent to parley before opening the door.   290

MR BUMBLE   *(Applying his mouth to the keyhole.)* Oliver!

YOUNG OLIVER   *(From inside.)* Come; you let me out!

MR BUMBLE   Do you know this here voice, Oliver?

YOUNG OLIVER   Yes.

MR BUMBLE   Ain't you afraid of it, Sir? Ain't you a-trembling while I speak, Sir?

YOUNG OLIVER   *(Boldly.)* No!

(MR BUMBLE steps back from the keyhole, draws himself up to his full height, and looks from one to another of the by-standers in mute astonishment.)   300

MRS SOWERBERRY   Mr Bumble, he must be mad! No boy in half his senses could venture to speak so to you.

MR BUMBLE   It's not madness, ma'am. It's meat.

MRS SOWERBERRY   What?

MR BUMBLE   Meat, ma'am, meat. You've over-fed him, ma'am. You've raised an artificial soul and spirit in him, ma'am, unbecoming a person of his condition: as the Board, Mrs Sowerberry, who are practical philosophers, will tell you. What have paupers to do with soul or spirit? It's quite enough that we let 'em have live bodies. It you had kept   310

unbecoming *'not suited to' Mr Bumble feels it is not right or decent that someone as poor as Oliver has been fed meat.*

the boy on gruel, ma'am, this would never have happened.

MRS SOWERBERRY Dear, dear! This comes of being liberal!

MR BUMBLE Ah! The only thing that can be done now, that I know of, is to leave him in the cellar for a day or so, till he's a little starved down; and then to take him out and keep him on gruel all through his apprenticeship. He comes of a bad family. Excitable natures, Mrs Sowerberry! Both the nurse and doctor said that that mother of his made her way here   32(against difficulties and pain that would have killed any well-disposed woman, weeks before.

(YOUNG OLIVER, hearing enough to know that some new allusion is being made to his mother, recommences kicking with a violence that makes every other sound inaudible. MR SOWERBERRY returns at this juncture.)

MRS SOWERBERRY He tried to murder poor Noah. We had to send for Bumble.

(MR SOWERBERRY unlocks the cellar door and drags out YOUNG OLIVER by the collar.)

MR SOWERBERRY Now, you are a nice young fellow, ain't you?   33(

(He gives YOUNG OLIVER a shake and a box on the ear.)

YOUNG OLIVER He called my mother names.

MRS SOWERBERRY Well, and what if he did, you little ungrateful wretch? She deserved what he said, and worse.

YOUNG OLIVER She didn't.

MRS SOWERBERRY She did.

YOUNG OLIVER It's a lie!

(That sends MRS SOWERBERRY into hysterics. Her flood of tears leaves MR SOWERBERRY no alternative, and he gives YOUNG OLIVER a sound drubbing, which satisfies even   34(MRS SOWERBERRY, and renders MR BUMBLE'S subsequent application of the parochial cane rather unnecessary.)

OLIVER
I bore the lash without a cry: for I felt that pride swelling in my heart which would have kept down a shriek to the last, though they had roasted me alive . . .

(MR and MRS SOWERBERRY, MR BUMBLE, CHARLOTTE and NOAH CLAYPOLe leave YOUNG OLIVER alone as the light fades. He falls on his knees on the floor.)

. . . But when there were none to see or hear me, I wept such tears as, God send, few so young may ever have had cause to pour out before me.

The candle was burning low in the socket when I rose to my feet. Having gazed cautiously around me, and listened intently, I gently undid the fastenings of the door and looked abroad. It was a cold, dark, sombre night, and I decided to leave that place for ever.

a cold, dark, sombre night *The three adjectives in succession makes this an effective description which reflects Oliver's feelings.*

INTERVIEWING: There is a dramatic and violent turn to this scene. Mrs Sowerberry bursts into tears and cries, 'What a mercy we have not all been murdered in our beds!'; Charlotte reports that Oliver almost killed Noah and that he thinks it necessary to call the army to restrain Oliver.

In groups of four take on the role of one of these four characters: Mr Bumble, Noah, Charlotte or Mrs Sowerberry.

Mr Bumble's role is to interview each character in turn about Oliver's attack on Noah. Each of the other characters should give his/her version of events with appropriate exaggeration.

DISCUSSION: When Oliver arrives at the Sowerberry's, he wishes he was dead and at the end of this scene he weeps bitterly.

In pairs select, discuss and list all the reasons for Oliver's misery you can find in the first two scenes of the play. Share your points with the rest of the class.

WRITING: Imagine that you are Oliver, alone after the thrashing Mr Sowerberry has given you. Write a diary entry covering your feelings about all that has happened at the Sowerberry's and expressing your determination to run away.

ACT 1 ❖ SCENE 3
BARNET

(The sun is rising in all its splendour, but the light only services to remind YOUNG OLIVER of his own loneliness as he sinks down, with bleeding feet, and covered with dust, upon a doorstep. A snub-nosed, flat-browed, common-faced boy, whom we shall know eventually as MR JACK DAWKINS – alias THE ARTFUL DODGER – passes him carelessly and then returns and surveys him most earnestly from the opposite side of the street.)

THE ARTFUL DODGER Hullo, my covey! What's the row? 1

(YOUNG OLIVER starts.)

THE ARTFUL DODGER Hullo, my covey! What's the row?

YOUNG OLIVER I am very hungry and tired. I have walked a long way. I have been walking these seven days.

THE ARTFUL DODGER Walking for sivin days! Oh, I see. You bin on the mill!

YOUNG OLIVER What mill?

A snub-nosed, flat-browed, common-faced boy *a detailed description of the Artful Dodger (using three compound adjectives in succession).*

covey *a form of 'cove' (fellow). The Dodger's speech is full of lively slang terms and lower class London pronunciation such as* **sivin** *for 'seven'.*

the mill *working the treadmill was a common form of punishment in Victorian England. The treadmill was a wheel enclosed in a cage. Prisoners operated this wheel by a constant and exhausting treading action on the steps of the wheel or 'endless staircase' as they termed it.*

THE ARTFUL DODGER	What mill! Why, the tread mill, eh! Beak's orders, you know.
YOUNG OLIVER	Beak? 10
THE ARTFUL DODGER	My eyes, how green can a man be? Why, a beak's a madgistrate. Where was you dragged up? All right! All right! Don't tell me yit! Eh! You 'ungry or sumpfin? You want grub? . . .
	(YOUNG OLIVER is almost too weak to nod.)
	. . . Right, you shall 'ave it. I'm at low water mark myself – only got a bob and a tanner, but I'll fork out, if ye're skint. Stay there . . .
	(YOUNG OLIVER tries to rise to his feet, but he has not succeeded before THE ARTFUL DODGER returns with a large ham roll. He gives this to YOUNG OLIVER, then he goes away again to fetch a half pint of beer.) 20
	. . . Going to London?
YOUNG OLIVER	Yes.
THE ARTFUL DODGER	Got any lodgings?
YOUNG OLIVER	No.
THE ARTFUL DODGER	Money?

Beak *a colloquial or slang term for* magistrate.

green *'naive and inexperienced'*

at low water mark *'short of money'*

a bob and a tanner *'an old shilling'* (five new pence) and *'sixpence'* (two and a half new pence).

skint *meaning* 'completely out of money', *a slang term in current use.*

YOUNG OLIVER	No . . .
	(THE ARTFUL DODGER whistles, and puts his arms into his pockets as far as his big coat sleeves will let them go.)
	. . . Do you live in London?
THE ARTFUL DODGER	Yus. I does when I'm at home. I suppose you want some place to sleep in tonight, doncher?
YOUNG OLIVER	I do, indeed. I have not slept under a roof since I left the country.
THE ARTFUL DODGER	Don't fret your eyelids on that score. I've got to be in London tonight; and I know a 'spectable old genelman as lives there, wot'll give you lodgings for nothink, and never ask for the change – that is, if any genelman he knows interduces you. And don't 'e know me? Oh, No! Not in the least! By no means. Certainly not. 'E'll give you a comfortable place to stay, as sure as my name is Jack Dawkins. C'm on. We'll 'ave to look slippy if we're to get to Islington before the ale 'ouses shut.

30

40

doncher *The Artful Dodger's pronunciation of* don't you.

to look slippy *'to move fast'*

EXPLORING LANGUAGE: This short scene is dominated by the lively language of The Artful Dodger.

In pairs pick out examples of the Dodger's language under the following headings:

	Accent	Slang	Imagery
E.g.	sivin	covey	green

IMPROVISATION: In pairs, improvise a modern version of this scene, in which a street-wise London teenager talks to a naive-looking runaway at the coach or railway station. Make sure you use modern slang terms.

ACT 1 ❖ SCENE 4
AT FAGIN'S

(A back room. The walls and ceiling of the room are black with age – it would be difficult to imagine a dirtier or more wretched place. Only a number of bright new or freshly washed silk handkerchiefs hanging over a clothes-horse relieve the monotony.

There is a shrill whistle from outside, followed by a knock. A very old shrivelled man comes in, his villainous-looking and repulsive face obscured by a quantity of matted red hair. He seems to be about to find out who whistled and knocked, then he hesitates, and goes back to the door through which he entered the room.)

FAGIN   *(Calling softly.)* Bates! Charley Bates! Come here, my dear, will you? . . .   1

(A young gentleman as rough as THE ARTFUL DODGER swaggers in, and he is followed by three or four more boys who are no older than he. All are smoking long clay pipes and drinking spirits with the air of middle-aged men.)

. . . There's some one at the door, Charley. See who it is, will you, my sweet?

(FAGIN fades into the background as CHARLEY BATES goes to answer the door.)

CHARLEY BATES	*(Calling out to the intruder.)* Now then.
A VOICE FROM BELOW	*(Giving the watchword.)* Plummy and slam!
CHARLEY BATES	*(Peering outwards and shading his eyes with his hand.)* There's two on you. Who's t'other one?
THE ARTFUL DODGER	*(Pulling YOUNG OLIVER forward.)* A new pal.
CHARLEY BATES	Where did he come from?
THE ARTFUL DODGER	Greenland. Is Fagin there?
CHARLEY BATES	Yes, he's a-sortin' the wipes. Come in!

(THE ARTFUL DODGER accepts the invitation. Then he sees FAGIN and goes to whisper a few words in his ear. Then he turns round and grins at YOUNG OLIVER. So, too, does FAGIN.) 3(

THE ARTFUL DODGER	This is him, Fagin. My friend Oliver Twist.
FAGIN	*(Making a low obeisance to YOUNG OLIVER, and taking him by the hand.)* My dear, I hope that I will have the honour of your intimate acquaintance . . .

(The young gentlemen with the pipes crowd round YOUNG OLIVER and shake his hands very hard – especially the one in which he still holds his little bundle. One young gentleman takes his hat and another saves him the trouble of emptying his own pockets. These civilities would probably be extended further, but for FAGIN'S liberal exercise of a toasting fork on the heads and shoulders of the affectionate youths who are offering them.) 4(

Plummy and slam! *the password needed to enter the thieves' den.*

Greenland *a joke about Oliver's innocence.*

wipes *'pocket handkerchiefs'*

obeisance *'an exaggerated bow'*

. . . We are very glad to see you, Oliver, very. Dodger, go and take off the sausages . . . Ah, you're a-staring at the pocket handkerchiefs! Eh, my dear! There are a good many of 'em, ain't there? We've just looked them out ready for the wash; that's all, Oliver; that's all! Ha! Ha! Ha! And now, my dears, you must git to your beds if you're going to see the fun at Newgate in the morning.

(The light fades, and FAGIN'S 'young gentlemen' go out.)

OLIVER   I slept, that night, on the floor, on a rough bed made of old   50
sacks . . .

(When the stage becomes light again, YOUNG OLIVER is lying in one corner of the room, and FAGIN is stirring some coffee in a saucepan and whistling softly to himself.)

OLIVER   It was late next morning when I awoke from a sound long sleep into that drowsy state between sleeping and waking in which one is half conscious of everything that is passing around, without being personally engaged.

FAGIN   *(To see if YOUNG OLIVER is awake.)* Oliver! Oliver Twist! My dear! . . .   60

(YOUNG OLIVER does not stir, so FAGIN produces a small box from some hiding place. He opens the box and takes from it a magnificent gold watch.)

. . . Aha! Clever dogs! Clever dogs! Staunch to the last! Never told the old parson where they were. Never peached upon old Fagin! And why should they? They wouldn't have loosened the knot, or kept the drop up, a minute longer. No, no, no! Fine fellows! Fine fellows! . . .

the fun at Newgate *a public hanging at Newgate, the notorious London prison demolished in 1802.*

the old parson *'the prison chaplain'*

peached upon *'informed against'*

(He pulls more jewellery from the box.)

. . . What a fine thing capital punishment is! Dead men   70
never repent; dead men never bring awkward stories to
light. Ah, it's a fine thing for the trade! Five of 'em strung
up in a row, and none left to play booty, or turn white-
livered! . . .

*(His bright dark eyes, which have been staring vacantly before
him, fall on YOUNG OLIVER'S face. Instantly, he closes the lid
of the box with a loud crash, and, laying his hand on a bread
knife, starts furiously up.)*

. . . What's that? What do you watch me for? Why are you
awake? What have you seen? Speak out, boy! Quick – quick!   80
For your life!

YOUNG OLIVER   *(Meekly.)* I wasn't able to sleep any longer, Sir. I am very
sorry if I have disturbed you, Sir.

FAGIN   You were not awake an hour ago?

YOUNG OLIVER   No! No, indeed!

FAGIN   *(With a threatening attitude.)* Are you sure?

YOUNG OLIVER   Upon my word I was not, Sir. I was not, indeed, Sir.

FAGIN   Tush, tush, my dear! Of course I know that, my dear. I only
tried to frighten you. You're a brave boy. Ha! ha! You're a
brave boy, Oliver! . . .   90

*(FAGIN rubs his hands with a chuckle, but he glances uneasily
at the box, notwithstanding.)*

. . . Did you see any of these pretty things, my dear?

(He lays his hand on the box.)

kept the drop up *'delayed the execution by preventing the opening of the
trap door on the scaffold'*

play booty and turn white-livered *'betray Fagin and turn coward'*

YOUNG OLIVER	Yes, Sir.
FAGIN	Ah! . . .

(He turns rather pale.)

. . . They're – they're mine, Oliver; my little property. All I have to live upon, in my old age. The folks call me a miser, my dear. Only a miser, that's all . . . Now, there's a pitcher of water in that corner by the door. Bring it here; and I'll give you a basin to wash in, my dear . . .   **100**

(YOUNG OLIVER walks across the room and stoops for an instant to raise the pitcher. When he turns, the box has gone.)

. . . Empty the basin out of the window, my dear, when you've finished . . .

(There is a shrill whistle outside. FAGIN hears the pass-words 'plummy and slam!', then he admits THE ARTFUL DODGER and CHARLEY BATES, who have been out on a foray.)

. . . Well! . . .   **110**

(He addresses himself to THE ARTFUL DODGER.)

. . . I hope you've been at work this morning, my dears?

THE ARTFUL DODGER	'Ard.
CHARLEY BATES	As nails.
FAGIN	Good boys, good boys! What have you got, Dodger?
THE ARTFUL DODGER	A couple of pocket-books.
FAGIN	Lined?

a foray *'a raid'*
pocket-books *'wallets'*

THE ARTFUL DODGER	Pretty well.
	(He produces two pocket-books.)
FAGIN	*(After looking at the insides carefully.)* Not so heavy as they might be, but very neat and nicely made. Ingenious workman, ain't he, Oliver?
YOUNG OLIVER	Very, indeed, Sir.
	(CHARLEY BATES laughs uproariously – very much to the amazement of YOUNG OLIVER, who sees nothing to laugh at in anything that has passed.)
FAGIN	*(To CHARLEY BATES.)* And what have you got, my dear?
CHARLEY BATES	*(Producing four pocket-handkerchiefs.)* Wipes.
FAGIN	*(Inspecting them closely.)* Well, they're very good ones, very. You haven't marked them well, though, Charley; so the marks shall be picked out with a needle and we'll teach Oliver how to do it. Shall us, Oliver, eh? Ha! Ha! Ha!
YOUNG OLIVER	If you please, Sir.
FAGIN	You'd like to be able to make pocket-handkerchiefs as easy as Charley Bates, wouldn't you, my dear?
YOUNG OLIVER	Very much, indeed, if you'll teach me, Sir.
	(CHARLEY BATES sees something so exquisitely ludicrous in this reply that he laughs until he is in danger of suffocation.)
CHARLEY BATES	Oh . . . oh . . . oh . . . He is so jolly green!
THE ARTFUL DODGER	*(Smoothing YOUNG OLIVER'S hair over his eyes.)* He'll know better, by-and-bye.

120

130

140

Ingenious *'skilful and clever'*

marks *laundry marks or initials by which stolen handkerchiefs could be traced.*

exquisitely ludicrous *'extremely funny and stupid'*

FAGIN

You watch our little game, Oliver. It's a jolly game, isn't it, boys? I'll put my snuff-box in here . . .

(He puts it in one pocket of his trousers.)

. . . a notecase in here . . .

(He puts it in the other pocket.)

. . . a watch in here . . .

(He puts it in his waistcoat pocket.)

. . . and a diamond pin in here . . .

(He sticks a mock diamond pin in his shirt.) 150

. . . Now, I'm a respectable old gentleman, out for a walk in the streets . . .

(He trots up and down the room with a stick.)

. . . You watch me . . .

(Sometimes he stops at the fireplace and sometimes at the door, making believe that he is staring with all his might into shop windows. THE ARTFUL DODGER and CHARLEY BATES follow him closely, getting out of his sight, so nimbly, every time he turns round, that it is impossible to follow their motions. At last, the ARTFUL DODGER treads upon his toes and CHARLEY 160 *BATES stumbles up against him behind, so that in one moment they take from him with the most extraordinary rapidity his snuffbox, notecase, shirt pin and pocket-handkerchief. Then FAGIN feels a hand in one of his pockets.)*

. . . Got you! Ain't I got you! Aha! Aha! Aha! There's a hand in my hip pocket there! I'll teach you! I'll teach you! I'll teach you!

(FAGIN picks up his toasting fork and starts to chase THE ARTFUL DODGER and CHARLEY BATES round the room. While he is doing this, BILL SIKES enters. SIKES, who is a 170 *stoutly built ruffian, is followed by NANCY, his girl.)*

37

BILL SIKES   What are you up to, eh? Ill-treating the boys, you covetous, avaricious, in-sa-ti-a-ble old fence? I wonder they don't murder you! I would if I was them. If I'd been your 'prentice, I'd have done it long ago, and – no, I couldn't have sold you afterwards, for you're fit for nothing but keeping as a curiosity of ugliness in a glass bottle, and I suppose they don't blow glass bottles large enough.

FAGIN   Hush! Hush! Mr Sikes! Don't speak so loud.

BILL SIKES   None of your mistering. You always mean mischief when   180
you come that. You know my name: out with it! I shan't disgrace it when the time comes.

FAGIN   Well, well, then – Bill Sikes. You seem out of humour, Bill.

BILL SIKES   Perhaps I am. I should think you was rather out of sorts, too, unless you means no 'arm by yer blabbing, and yer . . .

FAGIN   Are you mad?

(He catches BILL SIKES by the sleeve and points towards the boys. MR SIKES contents himself with tying an imaginary knot under his left ear, and jerking his head over on the right shoulder: a piece of dumb show which Fagin appears to   190 understand perfectly.)

. . . Here, boys . . .

(FAGIN produces a few shillings from some secret hiding place and gives them to the ARTFUL DODGER.)

. . . Go out and buy us some sausages – er, *beef* sausages, my

covetous *'wanting things belonging to other people'*

avaricious *'greedy'*

fence *'receiver of stolen goods'*

dumb show *Sikes is miming a hanging. It is now clear that some criminals known to Sikes and Fagin have been hung, that morning, at Newgate.*

dear – and anything else you fancy while I give Bill Sikes a glass of liquor.

(The boys take FAGIN'S money and go.)

BILL SIKES   And mind you don't poison it.

(FAGIN gets out liquor, and glasses, and gives a glass of spirits   200
to BILL SIKES, and one to NANCY.)

FAGIN   What do you want, Bill?

BILL SIKES   Blunt, you withered old fence, that's what I want – blunt. What the hell else do you think I would want?

FAGIN   Well, what have you brought me, my dear? . . .

(BILL SIKES produces, from a capacious inside pocket, a pair of silver candlesticks and a pair of silver salad servers. FAGIN inspects them closely.)

. . . Those aren't bad at all, Bill, they aren't bad at all.

BILL SIKES   Five pounds, I wants for 'em.   210

FAGIN   *(With a gesture of despair.)* Bill Sikes, you'll be the ruin of me! Two pounds, and not one penny more.

BILL SIKES   Give us 'em back, then. I'll take 'em where they're wanted.

FAGIN   Three, Bill . . .

(BILL SIKES shakes he head.)

. . . Three pounds three?

(BILL SIKES shakes his head again.)

. . . Three guineas?

(Another shake.)

Blunt *'cash' or 'ready money'*

... All right, then, Bill, I'll meet you. Three pounds four
shillings and sixpence. That's the right price, my dear.
That's all I'll get in the market.

BILL SIKES Well, if you won't give me any more, I suppose I must be
content with that. Come on. Hand over.

FAGIN I'll settle up when I see you next, Bill. I've just given the
boys money for sausages. I've only got eighteen-pence left
to keep house with.

BILL SIKES Come on, you old skinflint. You've got plenty more locked
away.

FAGIN I've got none to lock up, my dear – Ha! Ha! Ha! – None to
lock up. It's a poor trade, this one is, and no thanks; but I'm
fond of seeing the young people about me; and I bear it all,
I bear it all.

BILL SIKES That's all very well, Fagin, but I must have some blunt from
you before tonight.

FAGIN I haven't a piece of coin about me.

BILL SIKES Then you've got lots at the other ken. I must have some
from there.

FAGIN Lots! . . .

(He holds up his hands.)

. . . I haven't so much as would . . .

BILL SIKES I don't know how much you've got, and I dare say you
hardly know yourself, it'd take that long to count, but I
must have some tonight, and that's flat.

FAGIN Well, well. I'll send the Artful round, presently.

ken *thieves' slang for* hiding place *or* secret den.

220

230

240

BILL SIKES You won't do nothing of the kind . . .

(THE ARTFUL DODGER and CHARLEY BATES creep back into the room.)

. . . That Dodger's a deal too artful. 'Ed forgit to come, or lose his way, or get dodged by traps and so be prewented, or   250
anything for an excuse, if you put him up to it. No, Nancy shall go to the ken and fetch it, to make all sure – she'll be round while I'm 'aving my kip. Don't you fergit she's coming, will yer? Or else . . . C'mon.

(With a jerk of his head he signals to NANCY, who follows him out.)

THE ARTFUL Sausages, Fagin! . . .
DODGER

(He throws them across.)

. . . Beef sausages!

FAGIN Good boy! Good boy! Here! Here's two shillings! Now, you   260
and Charley go and enjoy yourselves! . . .

(THE ARTFUL DODGER and CHARLEY BATES take the money and make off.)

. . . There, my dear . . .

(FAGIN speaks to YOUNG OLIVER.)

. . . That's a pleasant life, isn't it? They have gone out for the day.

YOUNG OLIVER Have they finished work, Sir?

FAGIN Yes, that is, unless they should unexpectedly come across any when they are out: and they won't neglect it if they   270
do, my dear, depend upon it. Make 'em your models, my dear. Do everything they bid you, and take their advice in all matters – especially the Dodger's, my dear. He'll be a great man himself, and will make you one too if you take

pattern by him. – Is my handkerchief hanging out of my pocket, my dear?

YOUNG OLIVER Yes, Sir.

FAGIN See if you can take it out without my feeling it: as you saw them do when we were at play, just now . . .

(YOUNG OLIVER holds up the bottom of the pocket with one hand, as he has seen THE DODGER do, and he draws the handkerchief lightly out of it with the other.) 28

. . . Is it gone?

YOUNG OLIVER Here it is, Sir.

FAGIN *(Patting YOUNG OLIVER on the head approvingly.)* You're a clever boy, my dear. I never saw a sharper lad. Here's a shilling for you. If you go on in this way you'll be the greatest man of the time. And now come in here, and I'll show you how to take the marks out of the handkerchieves.

(He leads YOUNG OLIVER to the inner recesses of his den.) 29

OLIVER At the end of a month, I was reasonably proficient at the pocket-handkerchief game. By that time, I was beginning to languish, for want of fresh air, and I earnestly entreated the old gentleman, on many occasions, that he should allow me to go out to work with my two companions.

At length, one morning, I obtained the permission I had so eagerly sought. There had been no handkerchieves to work on for two or three days and the dinners at Fagin's had become, in consequence, decidedly meagre.

(FAGIN comes in, with YOUNG OLIVER. THE ARTFUL DODGER follows, with CHARLEY BATES.) 30

 take pattern by him *'model yourself on him'*

FAGIN	Oliver, here's a cap for you. I'm letting you go out this morning.
YOUNG OLIVER	Out?
FAGIN	Out. With the Dodger and Charley . . .
	(He turns to the other boys.)
	. . . I am letting you take young Oliver with you today, Dodger, and I want you and Charley Bates to keep a sharp eye on him. Bring him back safely, my dearest, or I'll C. . .H. . .U. . .C. . .K you down the S. . .T. . .A. . .I. . .R. . .S.

310

THE ARTFUL DODGER	Right you are, Fagin. Trust your old Dodger.
FAGIN	He's green, but he's . . .
	(FAGIN stops, as he sees the dark, cloaked figure of MONKS appear on the threshold.)
	. . . Mr Monks, Sir.
MONKS	A word with you, Mr Fagin, please.
FAGIN	Certainly, Mr Monks. I'll send the boys off, then we'll have some peace and quiet.
	(He makes a sign.)
THE ARTFUL DODGER	Come on, Oliver. Time to pad the hoof.

320

	(The boys go out. MONKS starts, when he sees YOUNG OLIVER.)
MONKS	That boy, Mr Fagin! Who is that boy?

to pad the hoof *'to be on our way', 'to get going'*

FAGIN	He's just a lad the Dodger found, Mr Monks. He has a very interesting history.
MONKS	His face seems oddly familiar to me, Mr Fagin. I think, perhaps, I might be very interested to hear that history. Will you share it with me?
FAGIN	For the right consideration, Mr Monks. Will you please to step this way?

(He leads MONKS off to his sanctum.)

330

OLIVER In spite of Fagin's admonitions The Artful Dodger and Charley Bates did not bring me back safely. They returned to Fagin's without me, very shortly after he had successfully got rid of his visitor Monks.

(FAGIN enters, with a pewter pot in one hand and the toasting fork in the other. There is a sausage on the end of the fork.)

FAGIN There's money in this for me. . . Big, big, money for me . . .

(There are footsteps on the stairs. He bends his ear towards the door and listens.)

340

. . . Here they are . . . *(His countenance changes.)*

. . . Why, how's this? Only two of 'em? Where's the third? They can't have got into trouble. Hark! . . .

(The footsteps reach the landing. The door is slowly opened; and THE ARTFUL DODGER and CHARLEY BATES come in.)

. . . Where's Oliver? Where's the boy? . . .

(The young thieves make no reply.)

. . . What's become of the boy? . . .

(FAGIN seizes THE ARTFUL DODGER tightly by the collar.)

. . . Speak out, or I'll throttle you . . .

350

(He shakes THE DODGER.)

. . . Will you speak?

THE ARTFUL DODGER	(*Sullenly.*) Why, the traps have got him, and that's all about it.
FAGIN	The traps have got him.
THE ARTFUL DODGER	We was on a prime plant, an old gent lookin' in at a bookstall, and just as we was right on 'is fogle, that Oliver must 'ave seen what we was up to and 'e started to 'op it. You should ha' 'eard the row they set up! 'Stop thief! Stop thief! Stop thief!', Yer never 'eard such a din. Like a pack of 'ahnds, they was. Well, 'e give 'em a good run, but they nabbed 'im at last, down by Clerkenwell Green, and Charley 'ere and I got clear away while they took 'im off to the Beak's Office. and now, let go o' me, will yer?

360

(With one jerk, THE ARTFUL DODGER swings himself out of his big coat, which he leaves in FAGIN'S hands. Then he snatches the toasting fork and make a pass at FAGIN with it. FAGIN seizes the pot of beer and hurls the contents at THE DODGER. The beer hits BILL SIKES, who has just come through the door, followed by NANCY.)

370

BILL SIKES	Why, what the blazes is this? Who pitched that 'ere at me? I might 'ave knowed as nobody but a rich, plundering old fence could afford to throw good drink away. Wot's it all about, Fagin?
FAGIN	The boy . . . Young Oliver . . . The traps have got him . . . He was out with the Dodger.
THE ARTFUL DODGER	It were a prime plant, too.
BILL SIKES	Well, what's ter that, eh? 'E won't git scragged.

traps *slang for 'police'.*

a prime plant *'an easy victim to pickpocket'*

fogle silk handkerchief *in thieves' slang.*

scragged *'hanged'*

FAGIN	I'm afraid that he may say something which will get us into trouble.

380

BILL SIKES	*(With a malicious grin.)* That's very likely. You're blowed upon, Fagin.
FAGIN	And I'm afraid, you see, if the game was up with us, it might be up with a good many more, and that it would come out rather worse for you than it would for me, my dear.
BILL SIKES	Somebody must find out wot's been done at the Beak's office . . .
	(FAGIN nods.)
	. . . If he hasn't peached, and is committed, there's no fear till be comes out again, and then he must be taken care on. You must get hold of him somehow.

390

FAGIN	*(Nodding again.)* You'll go, then, Mr Sikes?
BILL SIKES	Me? No. I ain't goin' near any Police office not fer anythink. Whaddya think I am?
FAGIN	Dodger?
THE ARTFUL DODGER	Not on your nelly. Cahnt me aht.
CHARLEY BATES	Nor me neither, Fagin.
FAGIN	Nancy will go; won't you, my dear?
NANCY	Wheres?

400

FAGIN	Only just up to the office, my dear.
NANCY	I'll be blessed if I will, Fagin, so it's no use a-trying that on.

 blowed upon *'informed against/exposed'*

46

BILL SIKES	What do you mean by that?
FAGIN	What I say, Bill.
BILL SIKES	Why, you're just the very person to go. Nobody about here knows anything of you.
NANCY	And as I don't want 'em to, neither, it's rather more 'no' than 'yes' with me, Bill.
BILL SIKES	She'll go, Fagin.
NANCY	No, she won't, Fagin.
BILL SIKES	Yes, she will, Fagin. Won't yer, Nancy? . . .

410

(He goes close to her and gives her a look that is full of significance.)

. . . Won't yer, Nancy?

NANCY	*(Submissively.)* Yes, Bill.
BILL SIKES	There's me dear.
FAGIN	Put this white apron on, Nancy . . .

(He ties an apron over her gown.)

. . . And this bonnet . . .

(He finds one from his inexhaustible stock.)

420

. . . Carry this in one hand . . .

(He gives here a little covered basket.)

. . . It looks more respectable, dear.

BILL SIKES	Give her a door-key to carry in her t'other one, Fagin. It looks real and genivine like.

genivine *'genuine'* or *'authentic'*

47

FAGIN	Yes, yes, my dear, so it does . . .
	(He hangs a street-door key on her forefinger.)
	. . . There, very good! Very good indeed, my dear!
NANCY	*(Feigning distress.)* Oh, my brother! My poor, dear, sweet, innocent little brother! What has become of him? Where have they taken him to? Oh, do have pity and tell me what's been done with the dear boy, gentlemen; do gentlemen, if you please, gentlemen!
	(She pauses, winks to the company, nods smilingly round, and disappears.)
FAGIN	Ah! She's a clever girl, my dears!
BILL SIKES	*(As they follow her out.)* She's an honour to her sex. Here's her health, and wishing they was all like her!

430

WRITING: A new and important character is introduced in this scene: Fagin.

Working in pairs, find all the detail you can about Fagin up to this point. Report your findings to the class and note the others' comments. Start a spider diagram on Fagin which you can add to as you read more of the play. For example:

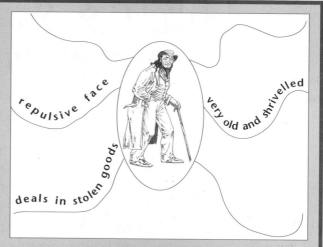

repulsive face

very old and shrivelled

deals in stolen goods

WRITING AND DISCUSSION: The secret password, 'Plummy and slam!' and the mention of Newgate Prison suggest that Fagin and the others are involved in crime. They also use slang terms about criminal activities. In the 19th Century, this was called thieves' slang.

In a pair, pick out as many terms of thieves' slang as you can find and try to explain their meanings.

For example: **wipes = handkerchiefs**

Discuss why it was necessary for thieves to have so many special and secret terms.

IMPROVISATION AND WRITING: Charley and The Dodger are nervous about telling Fagin that Oliver has been arrested.

In pairs, improvise their conversation after Oliver has been 'nabbed'.

Write a short script version of the improvised conversation between Charley and The Dodger. Include some of the 19th Century thieves' slang.

WRITING: Write a short account of the arrest of Oliver and the escape of the other two for *The Times* newspaper under the headline:

THE TIMES
London 20 October 1896

CHILD PICKPOCKETS CHASED

ACT 1 ❖ SCENE 5
AT MR BROWNLOW'S

OLIVER   But I had not been sent to prison. Struck by my strange
resemblance to a picture in his house – the likeness of a
poor girl who had been dead for many years – the old
gentleman refused to bring a charge against me, or to offer
any evidence. Instead, he took me to his home. There I was
bathed, and fed, and nursed through a fever – that assailed
me as a result of my privations.

They were happy days, those of my recovery. Everybody
was kind and gentle, and after the noise and turbulence in
the midst of which I had always lived, it seemed like
Heaven itself.

As soon as I was strong enough to put on a new suit of
clothes. Mr Brownlow, my benefactor, sent for me.

*(MR BROWNLOW is in his comfortable study. He tugs a bell-
pull, which brings MRS BEDWIN, his housekeeper, to him.)*

MR BROWNLOW   Ah, Mrs Bedwin, and how is young Oliver this evening.

MRS BEDWIN   Very happy, Sir, if I may say so, and very grateful indeed for
your goodness.

MR BROWNLOW   When he has finished his dinner will you be good enough
to ask him to step down here for a few minutes?

MRS BEDWIN   He's finished now, Sir. I'll go and tell him you want him.

*(She goes to fetch YOUNG OLIVER. In a moment the boy knocks
quietly on the door.)*

privations *'hardships'*
benefactor *Mr Brownlow paid to have Oliver looked after.*

MR BROWNLOW	Ah, Oliver! Come in a moment! Come in, and sit down! . . .
	(YOUNG OLIVER complies, and surveys with curiosity the shelves that reach from the floor to the ceiling.)
	. . . There are a good many books, are there not, my boy?
YOUNG OLIVER	A great number, Sir. I never saw so many.
MR BROWNLOW	You shall read them, if you behave well, and you will like that better than looking at the outsides – that is, in some cases; because there are books of which the backs and covers are by far the best parts . . .
	(YOUNG OLIVER smiles.)
	. . . How should you like to grow up a clever man, and write books, eh?
YOUNG OLIVER	I think I would rather read them, Sir.
MR BROWNLOW	What! Wouldn't you like to be a bookwriter?
YOUNG OLIVER	*(After a little consideration.)* I should think it would be a much better thing to be a book-seller, Sir.
MR BROWNLOW	*(To himself, having laughed at YOUNG OLIVER'S earnest answer.)* Curious instinct the young have for self-preservation . . .
	(He speaks to YOUNG OLIVER.)
	. . . Now, I want you to pay great attention, my boy, to what I am going to say. I shall talk to you without any reserve, because I am sure you are as well able to understand me as many older persons would be.
YOUNG OLIVER	*(Alarmed at MR BROWNLOW'S serious tone.)* Oh, don't tell me you are going to send me away, Sir, pray! Don't turn me out of doors to wander in the streets again. Let me stay here and be your servant. Don't send me back to the wretched place I came from. Have mercy upon a poor boy, Sir!

30

40

50

MR BROWNLOW	My dear child, you need not be afraid of my deserting you, unless you give me cause.
YOUNG OLIVER	I never, never will, Sir.
MR BROWNLOW	I hope not. I do not think you ever will. I have been deceived, before, in the objects whom I have endeavoured to benefit; but I feel strongly disposed to trust you, nevertheless. You say you are an orphan, without a friend in the world; all the inquiries I have been able to make confirm the statement. Let me hear the rest of your story; where you came from, who brought you up; and how you got into the company in which I found you. Speak the truth, and you shall not be friendless while I live.

(YOUNG OLIVER is about to start, when there is an impatient knock on the street-door. MRS BEDWIN comes to announce a visitor.)

MRS BEDWIN	It's Mr Grimwig, Sir.
MR BROWNLOW	Is he coming up?
MRS BEDWIN	Yes, Sir. He asked if there were any muffins in the house; and when I told him yes, he said he had come to tea.
MR BROWNLOW	*(To YOUNG OLIVER.)* This is a very old friend of mine, Oliver. You must not mind him being a little rough in his manners. He's worthy enough at heart.
YOUNG OLIVER	Shall I go downstairs, Sir?
MR BROWNLOW	No. I would rather you remained here.

(MR GRIMWIG walks into the room.)

| MR GRIMWIG | Look here! Do you see this! Isn't it a most wonderful and extraordinary thing that I can't call at a man's house but I find a piece of orange peel on the staircase. Orange peel! Orange peel will be my death, or I'll be content to eat my own . . . Hello! . . . |

(He notices YOUNG OLIVER, and retreats a pace or two.)

60

70

80

. . . What's that?

MR BROWNLOW	This is young Oliver Twist, whom we were speaking about.
	(YOUNG OLIVER bows.)
MR GRIMWIG	It that's not the boy, Sir, who had the orange, and threw this bit of peel upon the staircase, I'll eat my head, and his too.
MR BROWNLOW	*(Laughing.)* No, no, he has not had one. Come! Put down your hat; and speak to my young friend.
MR GRIMWIG	How are you, boy?
YOUNG OLIVER	A great deal better, thank you, Sir.
MR BROWNLOW	Step downstairs and tell Mrs Bedwin we are ready for tea, will you, Oliver?
YOUNG OLIVER	Certainly, Sir. *(He goes out.)*
MR BROWNLOW	He is a nice-looking boy, is he not?
MR GRIMWIG	*(Pettishly.)* I don't know.
MR BROWNLOW	Don't know?
MR GRIMWIG	No. I don't know. I never see any difference in boys. I only know two sorts of boys. Mealy boys, and beef-faced boys.
MR BROWNLOW	And which is Oliver?
MR GRIMWIG	Mealy. I know a friend who has a beef-faced boy; a fine boy, they call him; with a round head, and red cheeks, and glaring eyes; a horrid boy; with a body and limbs that appear to be swelling out of the seams of his blue clothes; with the voice of a pilot, and the appetite of a wolf. I know him! The wretch!

90

100

Mealy boys and beef-faced boys *'pale, unhealthy looking boys and red-faced, boisterous boys'*

pilot *one who guides a ship into harbour, calling out instructions as he does so. The implication is that the horrid boy has an over-loud and bossy voice.*

MR BROWNLOW	Come, these are not the characteristics of young Oliver Twist; so he needn't excite your wrath.

11

MR GRIMWIG	He may have worse. He may have worse, I say. Where does he come from? Who is he? What is he? He has had a fever. What of that? Fevers are not peculiar to good people, are they? Bad people have fevers sometimes; haven't they, eh? I knew a man who was hung in Jamaica for murdering his master. He had had a fever six times; he wasn't recommended to mercy on that account. Pooh! Nonsense!

(MRS BEDWIN comes in to lay a table for tea. She is followed by YOUNG OLIVER.)

MRS BEDWIN	May we come in, Sir?

12

MR BROWNLOW	Certainly, Mrs Bedwin.

(She starts to spread a table-cloth, helped by YOUNG OLIVER.)

MR GRIMWIG	*(With a certain amount of malice.)* And when are we going to hear a full, true and particular account of the life and adventure of Oliver Twist?
MR BROWNLOW	Oliver is in the middle of his account, my good friend, but I prefer that he shall be alone with me while he does so . . .

(He turns to YOUNG OLIVER.)

. . . Come up to me tomorrow morning at ten o'clock, my dear.

13

YOUNG OLIVER	Yes, Sir.

(There is a knock at the street-door. MRS BEDWIN goes to see who is there. YOUNG OLIVER follows her, so that he can help to carry in the tea-things.)

MR GRIMWIG	I'll tell you what. He won't come up to you tomorrow morning. I saw him hesitate. He is deceiving you, my good friend.
MR BROWNLOW	I'll swear he is not. I'll answer for that boy's truth with my life!

MR GRIMWIG	And I for his falsehood with my head!	**140**
MR BROWNLOW	We shall see.	
MR GRIMWIG	*(With a provoking smile.)* We will!	
	(MRS BEDWIN returns, with a small parcel.)	
MRS BEDWIN	It's the books you ordered, Sir.	
MR BROWNLOW	Ah, stop the boy, Mrs Bedwin. There is something to go back.	
MRS BEDWIN	He has gone, Sir.	
MR BROWNLOW	Call after him, will you? It's particular. He is a poor man, and they are not paid for. There are some books to be taken back, too.	**150**
	(MRS BEDWIN hurries out. In a moment she is back, followed by YOUNG OLIVER.)	
MRS BEDWIN	I'm sorry, Sir. He was right out of sight.	
MR BROWNLOW	Dear me, I am very sorry for that. I particularly wished those books to be returned tonight.	
MR GRIMWIG	Send Oliver with them. He will be sure to deliver them safely, you know.	
YOUNG OLIVER	Yes, do let me take them, Sir. I'll run all the way.	
	(MR BROWNLOW is just going to say that YOUNG OLIVER shall not go out on any account when a malicious cough from MR GRIMWIG causes him to change his mind.)	**160**
MR BROWNLOW	You shall go, my dear. Those are the books, over there . . .	
	(YOUNG OLIVER picks up the books that are to be returned.)	

malicious cough *Mr Grimwig makes a deliberate cough to show that he does not believe Oliver.*

	. . . You are to say that you have brought those books back, and that you have come to pay the four pound ten I owe him. This is a five-pound note, so you will have to bring me back ten shillings change.	
YOUNG OLIVER	I won't be ten minutes, Sir.	
	(He buttons up the bank-note in his jacket pocket.)	
MRS BEDWIN	Here's you cap, my dear, and your muffler . . .	17
	(She accompanies him to the door, fussing as she goes.)	
	. . . You mustn't catch cold. The evenings are very treacherous at this time of year.	
MR BROWNLOW	Let me see; he'll be back in twenty minutes, at the longest . . .	
	(He pulls out his watch.)	
	. . . It will be dark, by that time.	
MR GRIMWIG	Oh! You really expect him to come back, do you?	
MR BROWNLOW	Don't you?	
MR GRIMWIG	No! I do not. The boy has a new suit of clothes on his back, a set of valuable books under his arm, and a five-pound note in his pocket. He'll join his old friends the thieves and laugh at you. If ever that boy returns to this house, Sir, I'll eat my head.	18
MR BROWNLOW	Come up to the parlour, my friend. We'll watch for him.	

ten shillings *'fifty pence'*

muffler *'scarf'*

IMPROVISATION: In pairs, continue the conversation between Oliver and Mr Brownlow as though they had not been interrupted by Mrs Bedwin. Oliver tells the rest of his story and Mr Brownlow asks questions and expresses responses from time to time.

ACT 1 ❖ SCENE 6
A STREET

(YOUNG OLIVER is walking along, thinking how happy and contented he ought to feel, when NANCY appears and throws her arms tightly round his neck.)

YOUNG OLIVER Don't! Let go of me! Who is it? What are you stopping me for?   1

NANCY Oh my gracious! I've found him! Oh! Oliver! Oliver! Oh, you naughty boy, to make me suffer so! Come home, dear, come. Oh, I've found him. Thank gracious goodness heavins, I've found him! . . .

(A small crowd gathers, as NANCY becomes hysterical.)

. . . Come home directly, you cruel boy! Come!

FIRST BYSTANDER What's the matter, ma'am?

NANCY He ran away, near a month ago, from his parents, who are hard-working and respectable people; and went and joined a set of thieves and bad characters; and almost broke his mother's heart.   10

SECOND BYSTANDER Young wretch!

FIRST BYSTANDER Go home, do, you little brute!

YOUNG OLIVER I am not. I don't know her. I haven't any sister, or father or mother either. I'm an orphan; I live at Highbury.

NANCY Only hear him, how he braves it out!

YOUNG OLIVER Why, it's Nancy!

NANCY You see, he knows me! He can't help himself. Make him come home, there's good people, or he'll kill his dear mother and father, and break my heart!   20

BILL SIKES	*(Bursting out of a beer-shop.)* What the devil's this? Young Oliver! Come home to your poor mother, you young dog! Come 'ome, will yer?
YOUNG OLIVER	*(Struggling.)* I don't belong to them. I don't know them! Help! Help!
BILL SIKES	Help! Yus, I'll 'elp you, yer young rascal! What books is these? You've been stealing 'em 'ave yer? Give 'em 'ere.

(BILL SIKES tears the volumes from YOUNG OLIVER'S grasp and bangs the boy with them.)   3●

FIRST BYSTANDER	That's right! That's the only way of bringing him to his senses!
SECOND BYSTANDER	To be sure!
THIRD BYSTANDER	It'll do him good!
BILL SIKES	He shall have it, too! Come on, you young villain!

(He picks up YOUNG OLIVER, and carries him off.)

OLIVER	The gas-lamps were lighted; Mrs Bedwin waited anxiously at the open door; the servant ran up the street twenty times to see if there were any sign of my return; and still the two old 4● gentlemen sat, perseveringly, in the dark parlour, with the watch between them. They waited in vain.

WRITING: Oliver is the most important character in the play. He has appeared in every scene. Working in a group, collect evidence about Oliver from each scene of the play under the following headings:

	Feelings	Language	Actions	Character
E.g.	desperate with hunger (Sc.1)	speaks correctly and politely (Sc.2)	fights Noah calls Noah 'Sir' (Sc.2)	naive and innocent (Sc.3)

Write your own account of the character of Oliver in Act 1. Use the evidence you collected and noted in a group and read through your diary account before writing. Include references to what Oliver says and does and use quotations.

ACT 2 ❖ SCENE 1
THE MATRON'S ROOM, AT THE WORKHOUSE

(MRS CORNEY is about to make herself a pot of tea. At the fireplace, the smallest of all possible kettles is singing in the smallest of all possible voices.)

MRS CORNEY   Well, I'm sure we have all on us a great deal to be grateful   1
for! A great deal, if we did but know it. Ah! . . .

(The teapot, being very easily filled, runs over and the water slightly scalds MRS CORNEY'S hand.)

. . . Drat the pot! A little stupid thing, that only holds a couple of cups! What use is it to anybody! Except to a poor desolate creature like me. Oh, dear! . . .

(In her mind, there are awakened sad recollections of MR CORNEY who has been dead for more than five-and-twenty years.)   10

. . . I shall never get another! I shall never get another – like him! . . .

(There is a soft tap at the room-door.)

. . . Oh, come in with you! Some of the old women dying, I suppose. They always die when I'm at meals. Don't stand there letting the cold air in, don't. What's amiss now, eh?

THE VOICE OF MR BUMBLE   Nothing, ma'am, nothing.

MRS CORNEY   *(Her voice suddenly sweet again.)* Dear me! Is that Mr Bumble?

MR BUMBLE   At your service, Madam.

*(He now makes his appearance, bearing a cocked hat in one   20
hand and a bundle in the other.)*

MRS CORNEY	Hard weather, Mr Bumble.
MR BUMBLE	Hard, indeed, ma'am. Anti-porochial weather this, ma'am. We have given away, Mrs Corney, we have given away a matter of twenty quartern loaves and a cheese and a half this very blessed afternoon; and yet them paupers are not contented.
MRS CORNEY	Of course not. When would they be, Mr Bumble?
MR BUMBLE	I never see anything like the pitch it's got to. The day afore yesterday, a man – you have been a married woman, ma'am, and I may mention it to you – a man, with hardly a rag upon his back . . .

(MRS CORNEY looks modestly at the floor.)

	. . . goes to our overseer's door when he has got company coming to dinner; and says, he must be relieved, Mrs Corney. As he wouldn't go away, and shocked the company very much, our overseer sent him out a pound of potatoes and half a pint of oatmeal. 'My heart!' says the ungrateful villain, 'what's the use of this to me? You might as well give me a pair of iron spectacles!' 'Very good,' says our overseer, taking 'em away again, 'you won't get anything else here.' 'Then I'll die in the streets!' says the vagrant. 'Oh no, you won't,' says our overseer.
MRS CORNEY	Ha! Ha! That was very good! So like Mr Grannett, wasn't it? Well, Mr Bumble?
MR BUMBLE	Well, ma'am, he went away; and he did die in the streets. There's an obstinate pauper for you!
MRS CORNEY	It beats anything I could have believed!

30

40

---

quartern loaf *loaf weighing four pounds.*

the pitch it's got to *'the state it's reached'*

vagrant *'a tramp'*

MR BUMBLE	But these are official secrets, ma'am; not to be spoken of, except, as I may say, among the porochial officers such as ourselves . . . *(He stops to unpack his bundle.)*

50

. . . This is the port wine, ma'am, that the Board ordered for the infirmary; real, fresh, genuine port wine, only out of the cask this forenoon; clear as a bell; and no sediment!

(He holds the bottles up to the light, and shakes them well to test their excellence. Then he puts them down and takes up his hat, as if to go.)

MRS CORNEY	You'll have a very cold walk, Mr Bumble.
MR BUMBLE	*(Turning up his coat collar.)* It blows, ma'am, enough to cut one's ears off.

60

MRS CORNEY	Would you not care, Mr Bumble, for a little cup of tea?
MR BUMBLE	Why, thank you, ma'am, I don't mind if I do.

(He turns back his collar and lays his hat and stick upon a chair. Then he draws another chair up to MRS CORNEY'S table and sits down.)

MRS CORNEY	*(Taking up the sugar-basin.)* Sweet? Mr Bumble?
MR BUMBLE	Very sweet indeed, ma'am . . .

(He fixes his eyes on MRS CORNEY as he says this. She colours, as she passes him his tea.)

. . . You have a cat, ma'am, I see. And kittens too, I declare!   70

MRS CORNEY	I am so fond of them, Mr Bumble, you can't think. They're so happy, so frolicsome and so cheerful that they are quite companions for me.
MR BUMBLE	*(Approvingly.)* Very nice animals, ma'am. So very domestic.
MRS CORNEY	*(With enthusiasm.)* Oh, yes! So fond of their home, too, that it's quite a pleasure, I'm sure.
MR BUMBLE	Mrs Corney, ma'am, I mean to say this, ma'am; that any

cat, or kitten, that could live with you, ma'am, and not be fond of its home, must be a ass, ma'am.

MRS CORNEY Oh, Mr Bumble! 80

MR BUMBLE It's of no use disguising facts, ma'am, . . .

(He flourishes his teaspoon.)

. . . I would drown it myself, with pleasure.

MRS CORNEY *(Vivaciously.)* Then you're a cruel man . . .

(She holds out her hand for MR BUMBLE'S cup.)

. . . and a very hard-hearted man besides.

MR BUMBLE Hard-hearted, ma'am?

(He squeezes MRS CORNEY'S little finger.)

. . . Hard?

(He moves his chair round the table, to diminish the distance 90 *between himself and MRS CORNEY.)*

. . . Are you hard-hearted, Mrs Corney?

MRS CORNEY Dear me! What a very curious question from a single man. What can you want to know for, Mr Bumble? . . .

(MR BUMBLE drinks his tea to the last drop, wipes his lips, and deliberately kisses the matron.)

. . . Mr Bumble! Mr Bumble, I shall scream! . . .

(In a slow and dignified manner MR BUMBLE puts his arm round the matron's waist. Before she can scream, there is a loud knocking at the door, and her preparations are rendered 100 *unnecessary.)*

? **Vivaciously** *in a very lively and 'up-beat' manner.*

... Who's there?

(MR BUMBLE darts with great agility to the wine bottles and begins to dust them with great violence.)

FEMALE PAUPER *(At the door.)* If you please, mistress, Old Sally is a-going fast.

MRS CORNEY Well, what's that to me? I can't keep her alive, can I?

FEMALE PAUPER No, no, mistress. Nobody can; she's far beyond the reach of help. But she's troubled in her mind. She says she has got something to tell you which you must hear. She'll never die quiet till you come, mistress. 110

MRS CORNEY Ptchah! These old women! They can't even die without annoying their betters! ... *(She wraps herself in a shawl.)*

... Will you wait here, Mr Bumble? I'll be back presently ...

(She follows the FEMALE PAUPER, scolding all the way.)

... Make haste, will you? Don't be all night hobbling up them stairs!

IMPROVISATION: The story which Mr Bumble tells Mrs Corney about the vagrant who applied to the overseer for relief highlights the extremity of hardship. So hungry and destitute was this vagrant that he died of starvation.

In pairs, improvise in full the confrontation between the vagrant and the overseer.

WRITING: Write a short news report for national television news reporting the death of the pauper.

You could start, *'A homeless man died of starvation earlier today.'*

ACT 2 ❖ SCENE 2
THE INFIRMARY

(In a bare garret-room, OLD SALLY is dying. There is another old woman watching by the bed; the parish apothecary's apprentice is standing by its foot, picking his teeth with a quill.)

THE APPRENTICE   *(As MRS CORNEY enters.)* It's all U.P. here, Mrs Corney.

MRS CORNEY   It is, is it, Sir?

THE APPRENTICE   If she lasts a couple of hours, I shall be surprised. It's a break-up of the system altogether. Is she dozing, old lady?

(THE OLD WOMAN stoops over the bed, to ascertain, and nods. THE APPRENTICE drifts out.)

MRS CORNEY   *(To THE FEMALE PAUPER who has fetched her.)* She might last two hours. Did you hear that? How long do you expect me to wait?

THE FEMALE PAUPER   Not long, mistress. We have none of us long to wait for Death. Patience, patience! He'll be here soon enough for us all.

MRS CORNEY   Hold you tongue, you doting idiot! . . .

(She speaks to THE OLD WOMAN by the bed.)

. . . You, Martha, tell me; has she been in this way before?

THE OLD WOMAN   Often.

THE FEMALE PAUPER   She'll never wake again but once – and mind, mistress, that won't be for long.

---

apothecary *person who prepared and sold medicines; the forerunner of the modern chemist.*

U.P. *There is no hope left for Old sally; she is about to die.*

MRS CORNEY	*(Snappishly.)* Long or short, she won't find me here when she does wake; take care, both of you, you don't worry me again for nothing. It's no part of my duty to see all the old women in the house die – and what's more, I won't. Mind that, you impudent old harridans. If you make a fool of me again, I'll soon cure you, I warrant you!

20

(She is bouncing away, when there is a cry from the two women by the bed. OLD SALLY raises herself upright and stretches out her arms.)

OLD SALLY	Who's that?
THE OLD WOMAN	Hush, hush! Lie down, lie down!
OLD SALLY	I'll never lie down again alive! I will tell her! Come here! . . .

30

(OLD SALLY clutches MRS CORNEY by the arm.)

. . . Nearer! Let me whisper in your ear . . .

(She sees the two old women listening.)

. . . Turn them away. Make haste!

MRS CORNEY	Leave us, will you?

(The two old women move, protesting, to a place where they are apparently out of earshot.)

OLD SALLY	Now listen to me. In this very room – in this very bed – I once nursed a pretty young creetur' that was brought into the house with her feet cut and bruised with walking, and all soiled with dust and blood. She gave birth to a boy, and died. Let me think – what was the year again?

40

MRS CORNEY	*(Impatiently.)* Never mind the year! What about her?

harridan *'bad-tempered old woman'*

OLD SALLY	Ay, what about . . . what about . . . I know! I robbed her, so I did. She wasn't cold – I tell you, she wasn't cold, when I took it!
MRS CORNEY	Took what, for Goodness' sake?
OLD SALLY	The only thing she had. She wanted clothes to keep her warm, and food to eat, but she kept it safe, and had it in her bosom. It was gold, I tell you! Rich gold, that might have saved her life!
MRS CORNEY	Gold! Go on, go on – yes – what of it? Who was the mother? When did this happen?
OLD SALLY	She charged me to keep it safe, and trusted me as the only woman about her. They would ha' treated that child better, if they had known it all!
MRS CORNEY	Known what? Speak?
OLD SALLY	The boy grew so like his mother that I could never forget it when I saw his face. Poor girl! Poor girl! She was so young, too! Such a gentle lamb! Wait! There's more to tell. I have not told you all, have I?
MRS CORNEY	No! No! Be quick, or it may be too late!
OLD SALLY	The mother, when the pains of death first came upon her, whispered in my ear that if her baby was born alive, and thrived, the day might come when it would not feel so much disgraced to hear its poor mother named. 'And Oh, kind Heaven!' she said, folding her thin hands together, 'whether it be boy or girl, raise up some friends for it in this troubled world, and take pity on a lonely, desolate child, abandoned to its mercy!'
MRS CORNEY	The boy's name?

50

60

70

 wanted 'lacked'

OLD SALLY	They called him Oliver.
MRS CORNEY	Oliver!
OLD SALLY	The gold I stole was . . .
MRS CORNEY	Yes, yes – what?

(*MRS CORNEY is bending eagerly over to hear OLD SALLY's reply when the old woman clutches the coverlet, mutters some indistinct sounds in her throat, and falls lifeless. MRS CORNEY takes a scrap of paper from the dead woman's hand, and hides it.*)

80

THE FEMALE PAUPER	(*Hurrying back.*) Stone dead!
MRS CORNEY	And nothing to tell, after all.

(*THE MATRON walks carelessly back to her room, leaving the two crones to prepare for their dreadful duties.*)

crones *an unkind, insulting term for old women*

dreadful duties *The repeated 'd' sounds stress the grim nature of the women's task. They must prepare Old sally's body for burial.*

DISCUSSION: Oliver told us a little about his mother in the opening lines of the play, but Old Sally's account in this scene is more detailed.
In small groups, gather evidence from the opening lines of the play and from what Old Sally says about Oliver's mother.
For example: **She was pretty and young.**
Compare the evidence you have gathered with what Noah says about Oliver's mother in Act 1, Scene 4. Whose evidence are you more inclined to trust?

ACT 2 ❖ SCENE 3
THE MATRON'S ROOM

(MR BUMBLE is holding his own, private inventory of the contents of the room when MRS CORNEY hurries in, throws herself in a breathless state on a chair by the fireside, and gasps for breath.)

MR BUMBLE   Mrs Corney, what is this, ma'am? Has anything happened, ma'am? Pray answer me; I'm on – on –

(MR BUMBLE, in his alarm, cannot immediately think of the word 'tenterhooks'.)

. . . on broken bottles, ma'am.

MRS CORNEY   Oh, Mr Bumble! I have been so dreadfully put out!

MR BUMBLE   Put out, ma'am? Who has dared to . . . ? I know! This is them wicious paupers!

MRS CORNEY   It's dreadful to think of!

(She shudders.)

MR BUMBLE   Then don't think of it, ma'am.

MRS CORNEY   *(With a whimper.)* I can't help it.

MR BUMBLE   Then take something, ma'am . . . A little cup of wine?

MRS CORNEY   Not for the world! I couldn't . . . Oh! . . . The top shelf in the right-hand corner . . . Oh! . . .

(She points distractedly to a cupboard and then undergoes a convulsion from internal spasms. MR BUMBLE rushes to the closet, brings back a pint green-glass bottle, fills a teacup with its contents and holds the cup to the lady's lips.)

. . . I'm better now . . . It's peppermint. Try it! There's a little – a little something else in it . . .

(MR BUMBLE tastes the medicine with a doubtful look; smacks his lips; takes another taste; and puts the cup down empty.)

. . . It's very comforting.

MR BUMBLE   Very much so indeed, ma'am . . .

(He draws a chair beside the matron.)

. . . And now, ma'am, may I enquire what has happened to distress you?

MRS CORNEY   Nothing! I'm foolish, excitable, weak creetur'.

MR BUMBLE   *(Drawing his chair closer.)* Not weak, ma'am. Are you a weak   30
creetur, Mrs Corney?

MRS CORNEY   We are all weak creeturs.

MR BUMBLE   So we are . . .

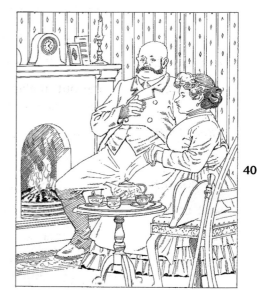

(Nothing is said, on either side, for a moment or two. By the end of that time, MR BUMBLE'S arm has become entwined with MRS CORNEY'S apron-string.)   40

. . . We are all weak creeturs . . .

(MRS CORNEY sighs.)

. . . Don't sigh, Mrs Corney.

MRS CORNEY   I can't help it. *(She sighs again.)*

MR BUMBLE   This is a wery comfortable room, ma'am . . .

(He looks round.)

. . . Another room, and this, ma'am would be a complete thing.   50

69

| MRS CORNEY | It would be too much for one. |
| MR BUMBLE | But not for two, ma'am? Eh, Mrs Corney? . . . |

(MRS CORNEY with great propriety turns her head away. She releases her hand to get at her pocket-handkerchief, but insensibly replaces it in that of MR BUMBLE.)

. . . The Boards allow you coals, don't they, Mrs Corney?

(He affectionately presses her hand.)

| MRS CORNEY | And candles. |

(She slightly returns the pressure.)

| MR BUMBLE | Coals, candles and house-rent free . . . Oh, Mrs Corney, what an Angel you are! . . . |

6

(MRS CORNEY sinks into MR BUMBLE'S arms. MR BUMBLE imprints a passionate kiss on her chaste nose.)

. . . Such porochial perfection! You know that Mr Slout is worse tonight, my fascinator?

| MRS CORNEY | Yes. |
| MR BUMBLE | He can't live a week, the doctor says. He is the master of this establishment; his death will cause a wacancy; that wacancy must be filled up. Oh, Mrs Corney, what a prospect this opens! What an opportunity for a jining of hearts and house-keepings! . . . |

7

(MRS CORNEY sobs.)

. . . The little word? The one little, little, little word, my blessed Corney?

---

propriety *'decency and correct behaviour'*

Coals, candles and house-rent free *These 'perks' (benefits of Mrs Corney's job) seem to be important in Mr Bumble's definition of angelic!*

fascinator *Mr Bumble means that he finds Mrs Corney very attractive. She commands his complete attention.*

MRS CORNEY	Ye-ye-yes!
MR BUMBLE	One more! Compose your darling feelings for only one more! When is it to come off?
	(MRS CORNEY twice essays to speak, and twice fails. At last, she summons up courage and throws her arms round MR BUMBLE'S neck.)
MRS CORNEY	It can come off as soon as you please, my love. You are an IR–RESISTIBLE DUCK!

80

WRITING: Working in pairs gather all the detail you can from this scene and from Act 1, Scene 1 about the possessions, prospects and personal qualities of Mr Bumble and Mrs Corney. Write a small ad. for each character for the 'lonely hearts' section of a local newspaper.

For example:

LONELY HEARTS ....

♥ FUN-LOVING widow with secure position as matron in workhouse seeks mature companion with view to com-

HOT-SEATING: Working in a small group, choose two people to take the parts of the female pauper from Scene 2, and Mr Bumble. Each character takes the hot-seat for two minutes to give his/her opinion of Mrs Corney and to answer questions. Which view of Mrs Corney is the more convincing?

ACT 2 ❖ SCENE 4
AT FAGIN'S

OLIVER

In spite of my pleas and prayers, Fagin would not allow me to send any message to Mr Brownlow, or to return the books, or in any other way to restore the old man's faith in me. Instead, I was kept a close prisoner at Fagin's for more than a month, being threatened, and cajoled, and told that I was ungrateful whenever my captor had a few moments to spare for hectoring me.

(FAGIN comes in, with YOUNG OLIVER.)

FAGIN

You was lonely, and hungry, and had nowhere to go when I took you in, is not that right, my dear? If it hadn't been for me, you might have perished with hunger. Well, what do you want to run away from your wery good friends for? I can't understand it, I just can't understand it. But you won't be trying it again, will you, my darling? Else you may finish up like a young lad I once took in here – such a nice young fellow – but was he grateful? Did he appreciate what I was doing for him? He . . .

(FAGIN lowers his voice.)

. . . He tried to peach on us, my dear. He tried to blab on the friends that had looked after him, that had filled his stomach and had given him a soft pillow for his head . . .

(FAGIN signs deeply, so that tears well into his kind old eyes.)

cajoled *'coaxed and flattered'*

hectoring *'bullying'*

peach *'inform on'*

blab *'tell the authorities'*

. . . Well, there was only one thing we could do, of course. We had to see that he was taken care of. There's such a thing as Crown Evidence, my dear – you may not have come across the words yet, but you will, you will . . . 'Crown Evidence', just you remember them . . .

(He sighs again, and shakes his head as he remembers the unfortunate young man who was so very disloyal.)

. . . They took him out one morning, just when Newgate Clock was striking eight. It isn't pleasant when they come for you that early, my dear. You've hardly had time to digest your breakfast in comfort before there's a knock on your door, and Mr Ketch is outside, with his assistants, and the Chaplain. He's a rough man is Mr Jack Ketch, my dearest . . .

30

YOUNG OLIVER *(Shuddering.)* Don't!

FAGIN He ties you up, so that his men can put you just where he wants you, on his trap.

YOUNG OLIVER Don't! Don't! Don't!

40

FAGIN And then he puts a horrid, stuffy black bandage over your eyes . . .

YOUNG OLIVER O-o-o-oh! *(With a long, shuddering cry YOUNG OLIVER runs away from FAGIN.)*

FAGIN We won't have much more trouble from that quarter, I imagine. He's a sensible child, is Young Oliver. He'll soon learn what is good for his health and what isn't.

(BILL SIKES comes up from the street, followed by NANCY.)

Crown Evidence *Fagin had fabricated evidence for the prosecution so that the young lad, who tried to talk to the police, was convicted and hung.*

Jack Ketch *Jack Ketch was a notoriously cruel public hangman from 1663 to 1683. Public hangings were common in Dickens's day and he wrote a famous account of a man who survived one by inserting a metal tube in his throat.*

BILL SIKES	Well!
FAGIN	Well, my dear – Ah, Nancy!
NANCY	Cold, Fagin?
FAGIN	It is cold, Nancy dear. It seems to go right through one.
BILL SIKES	It must be a piercer if it finds its way through your heart. Give him something to drink, Nancy. Burn my body, make haste! It's enough to turn a man ill, to see his lean old carcase shivering in that way, like a ugly ghost just riz from the grave.

50

(NANCY produces a large bottle of brandy from under her shawl and pours out a glass of it for FAGIN.)

FAGIN	*(Putting down the glass after just setting his lips to it.)* Quite enough, quite, thankye, Bill.

60

BILL SIKES	What? You're afraid of our getting the better of you, are you? Ugh . . .

(The burglar seizes the glass and throws its contents away. Then he fills it again, and tosses down the second glassful.)

. . . There! Now I'm ready.

FAGIN	For business?
BILL SIKES	For business. So say what you've got to say.
FAGIN	About the crib at Chertsey, Bill?
BILL SIKES	Yus. Wot about it?

7

FAGIN	Ah, you know what I mean, my dear. When is it to be done, Bill, eh? When is it to be done? Such plate, my dear, such plate!

---

carcase *Bill is sneering at Fagin's thin, pinched body by suggesting it is like the raw flesh of a dead animal.*

the crib *a house they intend to burgle.*

(FAGIN rubs his hands and elevates his eyebrows in a rapture of anticipation.)

BILL SIKES   *(Coldly.)* It ain't goin' to be done at all.

FAGIN   Ain't goin' to be done at all?

BILL SIKES   No. Leastways, it can't be a put-up job, as we expected.

FAGIN   *(Turning pale with anger.)* Then it hasn't been properly gone about. Don't tell me!   80

BILL SIKES   But I will tell yer. Who are you that's not to be told? I tells yer that Toby Crackit 'as been 'anging abaht the place for a fortnight, and 'e can't get none of the servants into a line.

FAGIN   *(With a deep sigh.)* It's a sad thing, me dear, to lose so much when we had set our hearts upon it.

BILL SIKES   So it is. Worse luck!

(He looks furtively at FAGIN.)

. . . Fagin! Is it worth fifty shiners extra if it's safely done from the outside?

FAGIN   Yes!   90

BILL SIKES   Is that a bargain?

FAGIN   Yes, my dear, yes!

BILL SIKES   Then let it come off as soon as you like. Toby and me were over the garden-wall the night afore last, a-soundin' the panels of the doors and shutters. The crib's barred up at night like a jail; but there's one part we can crack, safe and softly.

FAGIN   Which is that, Bill?

plate *expensive tableware, especially silver.*

a put up job *'robbery planned with inside help'*

shiners *'sovereigns'*

BILL SIKES	Why, as you cross the lawn . . .
	(He looks hard at FAGIN.)
	. . . Never you mind which part it is. You can't do it without me, I know; but it's best to be on the safe side when one deals with coves like you.
FAGIN	As you like, my dear, as you like. Is there no help wanted, but yours and Toby's?
BILL SIKES	None, 'cept a centre-bit and a boy. The first we've both got; the second you must find us.
FAGIN	A boy! Oh, then it's a panel, eh?
BILL SIKES	Never mind wot it is! I want a boy, and 'e mustn't be a big'un. Lord! If I'd only got that young boy of Ned, the chimbley-sweeper's! 'E kept 'im small on purpose and let 'im out by the job. But the farver gits lagged; and then the Juvenile Delinquent Society comes an' tikes the boy away from a trade where 'e was earnin' money, teaches 'im to read and write, and in time makes a happrentice on 'im; And so they goes on! If they'd got money enough, we shouldn't have half-a-dozen boys left in the 'ole tride in a year or two.
FAGIN	No more we should, no more we should . . .
	(An idea strikes him.)
	. . . Bill! What about Oliver?
BILL SIKES	Oliver? What Oliver?
FAGIN	Young Oliver Twist! He's the boy for you, my dear!

100

110

120

a centre-bit *a tool for drilling.*

lagged *'arrested and put in prison'*

The Juvenile Delinquent Society *A charitable institution founded in the first half of the 19th Century.*

BILL SIKES	Wot! 'Im?
FAGIN	Take him, Bill. I would, if I was in your place. He mayn't be so much up as any of the others, but that's not what you want if he's only to open a door for you.
BILL SIKES	Would 'e be sife?
FAGIN	I know he is, now. He's been in good training these last few weeks, and it's time he began to work for his bread. Besides, the others are all too big.
BILL SIKES	*(Ruminating.)* 'E's just the size I wants.
FAGIN	And will do everything you want, Bill, my dear. He can't help himself. That is, if you frighten him enough.
BILL SIKES	Frighten him! It'll be no sham frightening, mind yer. If there's anyfink bent abaht 'im when we once gits into the work you won't see him alive again, Fagin. You think on that, before you sends 'im.
FAGIN	I've thought of it all. I've had my eye on him, my dears – close, close. Once let him feel that he is one of us; once fill his mind with the idea that he has been a thief; and he's our's! Ours for his life. And, he'd better be. He knows too much about us now. He can shop us all if he tries giving leg-bail again. But it'll be quite enough for my power over him that he's been in a robbery. That's all I want. It couldn't have come about better.
NANCY	When's the job to be done, Bill?
FAGIN	Ah, to be sure. When is it to be done, Bill?

130

140

no sham frightening *'It won't be a case of pretending.'* Bill means what he says and will kill Oliver if necessary.

bent *'untrustworthy'*

giving leg-bail *'running away'*

BILL SIKES	I planned with Toby, the night arter tomorrer. If 'e 'eard nothink from me to the contrairy.

150

FAGIN	Good. There's no moon.
BILL SIKES	No.
FAGIN	It's all been arranged about bringing off the swag, is it? . . .

(BILL SIKES nods.)

. . . And about . . .

BILL SIKES	Oh, ah, it's all planned. Never mind the particulars. You go and git that boy. I wants ter get off the stones afore daybreak.

(FAGIN goes to fetch YOUNG OLIVER.)

FAGIN	Come, my dear, you're going on a nice little journey into the country with Mr Sikes.

160

YOUNG OLIVER	*(Anxiously.)* To – to – stop there, Sir?
FAGIN	No, no, my dear. Not to stop there. We shouldn't like to lose you. Don't be afraid, Oliver, you shall come back to us again. Ha! Ha! Ha!. We won't be so cruel as to send you away, my dear, Oh no! No! . . .

(He looks round furtively.)

. . . I suppose you want to know what you are going with Bill for, eh, my dear?...

(YOUNG OLIVER nods his head.)

170

. . . Why, do you think?

YOUNG OLIVER	Indeed I don't know, Sir.

swag *'stolen goods'*
get off the stones *'get out of London'*
furtively *'stealthily'*

FAGIN   Bah! Wait till Bill tells you, then . . .

(He hesitates, and then puts a warning hand on YOUNG OLIVER'S arm.)

. . . Take heed, Oliver! Take heed! He's a rough man, and thinks nothing of blood when his own is up. Whatever falls out, say nothing; and do what he bids you. Mind!

(With a final admonitory wag of his forefinger, FAGIN leaves YOUNG OLIVER alone.)   180

OLIVER   But Bill's instructions, when they came, were not particularly informative.

BILL SIKES   Come 'ere young 'un, and let me read you a lectur', which is as well got over at once . . .

(YOUNG OLIVER stands in front of BILL SIKES, who takes up a pocket-pistol.)

. . . Now, first: do you know wot this is? . . .

(YOUNG OLIVER nods his head.)

. . . Well, then, look here. This is powder; that 'ere's a bullet; and this is a little bit of a old 'at, fer waddin' . . .   190

(BILL SIKES proceeds to load the pistol, with great nicety and deliberation.)

. . . Now it's loaded.

YOUNG OLIVER   Yes, I see it is, Sir.

BILL SIKES   Well, if you speak a word when you're out o'doors wi' me, except when I speaks ter you, that loading will be in yer 'ead without notice. So, if you do make up yer mind to

when his own is up *'when he is in a temper'*

admonitory *'warning'*

nicety *'precision'*

speak without leave, say yer prayers first . . .

(BILL SIKES scowls at YOUNG OLIVER to increase the effect of his warning.)

200

. . . As near as I know, there ain't anybody as would be askin very partickler arter you, if you was disposed of; so I needn't take this devil-and-all of trouble to explain matters to yer, if it warn't fer your own good. D'ye hear me? . . .

(YOUNG OLIVER nods.)

. . . And now, let Nancy take 'ee off and give 'ee a good bellyful of scoff before we sets out. It'll be quite a long time, before we're both back.

NANCY   *(As she takes YOUNG OLIVER off for food.)* You'll be all right, my dear, as long as you don't cross him. If you do, 'ell stop you telling tales for ever arterwards, and 'ell take 'is chance of swingin' for it. C'mon. I expect you're 'ungry.

210

OLIVER   But you didn't shoot me, did you, Bill Sikes?

BILL SIKES   Nah. That wasn't the way it worked out at all. When we got to the crib we was goin' ter crack, I showed you a little lattice window, remember?

OLIVER   I remember.

BILL SIKES   And Flash Toby and I put yer through it, remember that too?

OLIVER   How could I forget? You told me you'd give me a crack on the head with your gun if I didn't do exactly as you told me.

220

BILL SIKES   And do yer wonder? Yer was prayin' ter all the Bright

bellyfull of scoff *lively slang expression for a good meal.*

lattice window *A leaded window with small diamond shaped panes.*

Angels in 'Eaven ter 'ave mercy on yer. We only wanted yer to undo the street door and let us in.

OLIVER But I didn't get a chance, did I? Almost as soon as I got my feet on the scullery floor I dropped the lantern I was carrying . . .

BILL SIKES That brought the two men servants to the top of the stairs, blast yer . . . 230

OLIVER Everything swam in front of my eyes . . .

BILL SIKES There was a flash . . .

OLIVER A loud noise . . .

BILL SIKES It knocked Toby and me flat backwards, tip over tail . . .

OLIVER There was smoke everywhere . . .

BILL SIKES But we got yer by the collar, and dragged yer back . . .

OLIVER I can remember the loud ringing of a bell, mingled with the noise of firearms . . .

BILL SIKES There was men shoutin', everywhere . . .

OLIVER And I felt as if I was being carried over uneven ground at a rapid pace. 240

BILL SIKES You was. By me.

OLIVER But then the noises grew confused in the distance.

BILL SIKES You was feelin' faint, more as like. I 'ad you 'ead dahnwards over me shoulder.

OLIVER And I remember no more.

BILL SIKES That's 'cos I 'ad to drop yer dahn in a dry ditch when the chase got too 'ot. Yer was like deff itself, when I left yer.

OLIVER But, somehow, I found my way back to the house you had taken me to rob. I pushed against the garden-gate, tottered across the lawn, climbed the steps, knocked faintly on the 250 door, and, my whole strength failing me, sank down against one of the pillars of the little portico.

BILL SIKES   By that time, o'course, Toby and me was 'arf way back to London.

(BILL lurches off.)

portico *a series of columns along the side of a building.*

AT FAGINS – after Fagin leaves Young Oliver alone – up to page 73

DISCUSSION: Fagin makes his second appearance in the play in this scene. No new detail is given about him directly but we learn more about his character from what he says and plans to do.

In small groups discuss what we learn about Fagin in this scene. Add detail to your spider diagram on his character.

EXPLORING LANGUAGE: In pairs add any new terms of thieves' slang you can find, up to this point in the scene, to the list you began after Act 1, Scene, 4.

AT FAGINS – (from page 80 to end of scene)

ROLE PLAY: In groups of three prepare and practise a television or radio news item on the attempted robbery at Chertsey, making careful use of detail given in the script. One student should take the role of news presenter and give an outline of the crime. The other two should take on the roles of interviewer and of Oliver.

ACT 2 ❖ SCENE 5
AT THE WORKHOUSE, AGAIN

(MR BUMBLE comes in and sits down in the Matron's parlour. He rests his eyes moodily on the cheerless grate, though he raises them occasionally to look at a paper fly-cage that dangles from the ceiling. The sight depresses him deeply, reminding him, as it does, of his present unhappy condition.)

MR BUMBLE	*(With a sigh.)* And tomorrow two months it was done! It seems a hage . . .	1

(He closes his eyes for a moment, as if he can bear no longer the sight of captured flies.)

. . . I sold myself for six teaspoons, a pair of sugar-tongs, and a milk-pot; with a small quantity of second-hand furniture, and twenty pound in money. I went very reasonable. Cheap, dirt cheap!

MRS BUMBLE	*(Materialising almost from nowhere.)* Cheap! You would have been dear at any price; and dear enough I paid for you, Lord above knows that!	10
MR BUMBLE	*(Turning suddenly.)* Mrs Bumble, ma'am!	
MRS BUMBLE	Well?	
MR BUMBLE	Have the goodness to look at me.	
MRS BUMBLE	Look at you? Hah! Oh, hah! . . .	

(MR BUMBLE, finding that his pauper-quelling eye is powerless against MRS BUMBLE, relapses into gloom.)

. . . Well? Are you going to sit snoring there all day?

MR BUMBLE	I am going to sit here, as long as I think proper, ma'am; and although I was *not* snoring, I shall snore, gape, sneeze,	20

	laugh, or cry, as the humour strikes me; such being my prerogative.
MRS BUMBLE	*(With ineffable contempt.)* Your prerogative!
MR BUMBLE	I said the word, ma'am. The prerogative of a man is to command.
MRS BUMBLE	And what's the prerogative of a woman, in the name of Goodness?
MR BUMBLE	To obey, ma'am. Your late unfortunate husband should have taught it you; and then, perhaps, he might have been alive now. I wish he was, poor man! . . .

(MRS BUMBLE sees that the decisive moment has now arrived, and that a blow struck for mastership at this point must necessarily be final and conclusive. She drops into a chair, accuses MR BUMBLE with a loud scream of being a hard-hearted brute, and falls into a paroxysm of tears.)

MR BUMBLE *(Whose heart is water-proof.)* Cry on, my sweetest. I beg you, cry your hardest. The practice is looked on, they say, has being 'ighly conducive to 'ealth. It opens the lungs . . .

(A howl, from MRS BUMBLE.)

. . . It washes the countenance, it exercises the eyes, and softens down the temper. So cry away, me loving poppet, cry away.

(MR BUMBLE puts on his hat at a rakish angle and, having asserted his superiority, and the superiority of all males, so effectively, he saunters towards the door.

But MRS BUMBLE has only tried tears because they are less

---

ineffable contempt *Mrs Bumble's scorn for her husband is stronger than words can suggest.*

prerogative *'right'*

---

troublesome, for her, than a manual assault. Before
MR BUMBLE can escape she sends his hat flying suddenly to the
opposite end of the room. Then she clasps him tightly round the
throat with one hand and inflicts condign punishment on him,   50
in a highly expert way, with the other. Finally, she pushes him
over a chair.)

MRS BUMBLE   Prerogative! Prerogative! Just mention that word again if
you dare! And now, get up! And take yourself away from
here, unless you want me to do something desperate! . . .

(MR BUMBLE rises with a very rueful countenance, wondering
what something desperate may be. He picks up his hat and looks
towards the door.)

. . . Are you going?

MR BUMBLE   Certainly, my dear, certainly. I didn't intend to . . . I'm   60
going, my dear! You are so very violent, that really I . . .

(MRS BUMBLE steps hastily forward to replace the carpet, which
has been kicked up in the scuffle. MR BUMBLE immediately
darts to a position of safety out of her range.

While he is recovering his breath, and his equilibrium, he is
approached by a mysterious stranger. It is MR MONKS, whom
we last saw at FAGIN'S.)

MR MONKS   Excuse me, Sir, do you happen to be the beadle here?

MR BUMBLE   I was, young man, I was. The Porochial Beadle. But now I
am the Master of the Workhouse. The Master of the   70
Workhouse, young man!

---

a manual assault *laying her hands on him in a violent manner*

condign *'fitting and well-deserved'*

rueful countenance *'looking sorry and upset'*

equilibrium *'balance and composure'*

MR MONKS	You have an eye to your own interest, I doubt not? Don't scruple to answer freely, man.
MR BUMBLE	I suppose, a married man is not more averse to turning an honest penny when he can than a single one. Porochial officers are not so well paid that they can afford to refuse any extra fee when it comes to them in a civil and proper manner.
MR MONKS	I want some information from you. I don't ask you to give it for nothing, slight as it is. Put up that, to begin with . . .

(He hands two sovereigns to MR BUMBLE, who examines them scrupulously to see that they are genuine, and then puts them with much satisfaction in his waistcoat-pocket.)

. . . Carry your memory back – let me see – twelve years last winter.

MR BUMBLE	It's a long time . . . Very good, I've done it.
MR MONKS	The scene, the workhouse.
MR BUMBLE	Good!
MR MONKS	And the time, night.
MR BUMBLE	Yes.
MR MONKS	The place, the crazy hole where miserable drabs give birth to puling children for the parish to rear.

scruple *'hesitate'* or *'worry about'*

not more averse to turning an honest penny *in favour of making some money 'on the side'.*

twelve years last winter *Monks is referring to the birth of Oliver. More than three years have passed since the opening scene when Mr Bumble mentioned Oliver's ninth birthday.*

drabs *'prostitutes'*

puling *'whining and sickly'*

MR BUMBLE	*(Not quite following.)* The lying-in room, I suppose?
MR MONKS	Yes. A boy was born there.
MR BUMBLE	A many boys.
	(He shakes his head despondingly.)
MR MONKS	I speak of one: a meek-looking, pale-faced boy, who was apprenticed down here to a coffin-maker, and who afterwards ran away to London, as it is supposed.
MR BUMBLE	Why, you mean Oliver! Young Twist! I remember him, of course. There wasn't an obstinater young rascal . . .
MR MONKS	It's not of him I want to hear. It's of a woman; the woman that nursed his mother. Where is she?
MR BUMBLE	Where is she? It would be hard to tell. There's no midwifery there, whichever place she's gone to.
MR MONKS	What do you mean?
MR BUMBLE	She died last winter.
	(MR MONKS draws in his breath sharply.)
MR MONKS	It's no great matter. And now, I have a long way to go.
MR BUMBLE	Wait! My wife . . . The Workhouse Master's wife . . . She was with Old Sally, if I remember haright, on the evening she died. I have reason to believe that Old Sally may have told her something.
	(He walks across to MRS BUMBLE, who has been well aware of what has been going on.)
	. . . My dear . . .

100

110

The lying-in room *'the room in which women give birth'*

midwifery *The job of helping at the birth of babies.*

(He whispers in her ear, then she nods her head, then he goes across to MR MONKS and leads him to MRS BUMBLE.)

MR MONKS Madam, I believe you were with a certain old woman of this workhouse when she died . . .

(MRS BUMBLE inclines her head.)

. . . Your husband tells me that she may have told you something . . .

MRS BUMBLE About the mother of a certain boy we once had here. Yes.

MR MONKS The first question is, of what nature was her communication?

MRS BUMBLE That's the second question. The first is, what may the communication be worth?

MR MONKS Hah! There may be money's worth to get, eh?

MRS BUMBLE Perhaps there may.

MR MONKS Something that was taken from her? Something that she wore? Something . . .

MRS BUMBLE *(Interrupting.)* You had better make me an offer. I've heard enough already to tell me you're the man I ought to talk to. What's it worth to you?

MR MONKS It may be nothing; it may be twenty pounds. Speak out, and let me know which.

MRS BUMBLE Give me five-and-twenty pounds in gold, and I'll tell you all I know. Not before.

MR MONKS Five and twenty pounds!

MRS BUMBLE I spoke as plainly as I could. It's not a large sum, either.

MR MONKS Not a large sum for a paltry secret that may be nothing when it's told?

MRS BUMBLE You can easily take it away again. I am but a woman; alone here; unprotected.

12

13

14

MR BUMBLE	Not alone, my dear, nor unprotected neither . . .
	(His teeth chatter as he speaks.)
	. . . I am here, my dear. And, besides, Mr Monks is too much of a gentleman to attempt any violence on porochial persons. Mr Monks is aware that I am not a young man, my 150 dear, and also that I am a little run to seed, as I may say; but he has heerd: I say I have no doubt Mr Monks has heerd, my dear: that I am a very determined officer, with very uncommon strength, if I'm once roused. I only want a little rousing, that's all.
MRS BUMBLE	You're a fool; and you'd better hold your tongue.
	(MR MONKS produces a canvas bag and counts out twenty-five sovereigns.)
MR MONKS	There are the sovereigns. Now, let's hear your story.
MRS BUMBLE	When this woman, that we called Old Sally, died, she and I 160 were alone.
MR MONKS	Good. Go on.
MRS BUMBLE	She spoke of a young creature who had brought a child into the world some years before; not merely in the same room, but in the same bed in which she lay dying. The child was the boy you named. The mother, Old Sally had robbed.
MR MONKS	In life?
MRS BUMBLE	In death. She stole from the corpse something that the dying mother had prayed her, with her last breath, to keep for the infant's sake. 170

paltry *'trashy'*

run to seed *'past his best in strength and energy'*

a young creature *Mrs Bumble uses standard forms of the language when she is discussing an important matter with a social superior:* **creature** *rather than* **creetur**.

MR MONKS	She sold it? Did she sell it? Where? When? To whom? How long before?
MRS BUMBLE	When Old Sally died, I found in her hand a scrap of dirty paper.
MR MONKS	Which contained?
MRS BUMBLE	Nothing. It was a pawnbroker's ticket.
MR MONKS	For what?
MRS BUMBLE	She must have kept the trinkets she took from the dying woman for some time, in the hope of turning them to better account. Then, she must have pawned them. Each year, she must have saved or scraped enough money together to pay the pawnbroker's interest, and prevent its running out; so that if anything came of the matter the trinkets could still be redeemed. Nothing had come of it; and, as I tell you, she died with the scrap of paper, all worn and tattered, in her hand. The time was out in two days; I thought something might one day come of it, too; and so I redeemed the pledge.
MR MONKS	Where is it now?
MRS BUMBLE	There!

(She hands across a small kid bag, which MR MONKS pounces upon, and tears open.)

MR MONKS	*(As he inspects the contents of the bag.)* A gold locket . . . Yes! . . . A plain gold wedding ring . . . Yes! . . . With 'Agnes' engraved on the inside, and a blank left for the surname . . . Then follows the date . . . And is this all?
MRS BUMBLE	All. Is it what you expected to get from me?

pawnbroker *A dealer who lends money out on goods.*

redeemed *'bought back'*

MR MONKS   It is . . .

(He puts the bag carefully away in his pocket.)

. . . And now, we can have nothing more to say, and may
break up our pleasant party.   200

DISCUSSION: Mr Monks appears in the play for the second time in
this scene. He is clearly linked to some mystery surrounding Oliver
and his mother. There have been a number of clues in the play so far
about the identity of Oliver and his mother.

In small groups, list evidence concerning Oliver's identity after looking back
over the following sections of the play:
Act 1, Scene 4 – *Monks catches sight of Oliver.*
Act 1, Scene 5 – *Oliver is struck by a picture at Mr Brownlow's*
Act 2, Scene 2 – *Old Sally's dying words*
Act 2, Scene 5 – *Monks and Mrs Bumble*

In your group try to work out why Monks is so interested in Oliver's mother and
suggest the identity of Oliver. Share your ideas with the rest of the class.

DISCUSSION: In a pair, decide which partner has the upper hand in the Bumble
marriage. List the evidence which supports your decision. E.g.: Mrs Bumble calls
her husband a 'fool', and tells him to 'hold his tongue'.

WRITING: The first part of this scene shows that all is not happy in the Bumble
marriage.
    In a pair write:
    1   a letter from Mr Bumble to an agony aunt or uncle describing the state of
        his marriage and requesting advice.
    2   The reply from the agony aunt or uncle.

ACT 2 ❖ SCENE 6
FAGIN'S

(Darkness. There is a faint glimmer of a lantern, and then a low whistle. The whistle is repeated.)

THE ARTFUL DODGER	*(In a whisper.)* Now then?
TOBY CRACKIT	*(In a whisper.)* Plummy and slam!
THE ARTFUL DODGER	Come on in. Wait there. *(THE ARTFUL DODGER moves away and whispers mysteriously to FAGIN.)*
FAGIN	What, alone?
THE ARTFUL DODGER	Yus.
FAGIN	Where is he?
THE ARTFUL DODGER	Out there.
FAGIN	Bring him in. Hush! Quiet, Charley! Gently, Tom! Scarce! Scarce!

(The boys, hidden in the shadows, disperse.)

TOBY CRACKIT	How are you, Faguey? . . .

(FAGIN grips him by the collar.)

. . . Don't look at me in that way, man. All in good time. I can't talk business till I've eat and drank, so produce some scoffer, will yer? I ain't 'ad nuffin, 'ardly, these three days and nights.

FAGIN	The Dodger'll get some grub presently. Here's some gin, my dearest. Get that inside you. Then you'll be ready for talking.

TOBY CRACKIT	*(TOBY CRACKIT drinks.)* Tchah! That's better. Now, first and foremost, Faguey, how's Bill?
FAGIN	*(A scream.)* WHAT?
TOBY CRACKIT	Why, you don't mean to say . . .
FAGIN	Mean? Where are they? Sikes and the boy! Where are they? Where have they been? Where are they hiding? Why have they not been here?
TOBY CRACKIT	*(Faintly.)* The crack failed.
FAGIN	Failed?
TOBY CRACKIT	They fired and hit the boy. We cut over the fields at the back, with him between us . . . straight as the crow flies . . . through 'edge and ditch. They gave chase. Damme! The whole country was awake, and the dogs upon us.
FAGIN	The boy?
TOBY CRACKIT	Bill 'ad 'im on 'is back, and scudded like the wind. We stopped to take 'im between us; 'is 'ead 'ung down, and 'e was cold. They were close upon our 'eels; every man for 'imself, and each from the gallows! We parted company, and left the youngster lying in a ditch. Alive or dead, that's all I know about 'im . . .
	(FAGIN utters a loud yell, and wrings his hands.)
	. . . Though I did 'ear tell, in two of the ale 'ouses I stopped at, that the boy 'ad gone back to the crib, and 'ad been taken in, and was being looked arter by the fambly.
FAGIN	Oy! . . . Oy! . . . Oy! . . . Oh, why should this happen to

30

40

---

scoffer *slang for 'food'.*

crack *'break-in'*

scudded *'swept along very swiftly'*

me? . . . *(He hears the soft sound of a footstep.)*

. . . Go through to the back, my dearest. The Dodger will give you your grub . . .

(FAGIN has hardly ushered TOBY CRACKIT out, before MONKS appears, in the other doorway.)

MONKS   Fagin!

FAGIN   *(Turning quickly round.)* Ah! Is that . . .

MONKS   Yes! I have been waiting for you for hours. Where the devil have you been?

FAGIN   On your business, my dear. On your business all night.

MONKS   *(With a sneer.)* Oh, of course! Well; and what's come of it?

FAGIN   Nothing good.

MONKS   Nothing bad, I hope? . . . *(He looks round.)*

              . . . Can anyone hear?

FAGIN   Not a living soul. Toby Crackit's in the back room having his grub, and the boys are with him.

MONKS   And Oliver?

FAGIN   Oliver's at Chertsey, still. I sent him out on a crack with Bill Sikes, and the crack failed. They scarpered, across country, but Bill had to drop the boy when the pace got too hot. Flash Toby Crackit has heard he went back to the crib. Taken in and made much of, he said. It was the talk of the ale-houses as he came through.

MONKS   Damnation to you, Fagin! . . . *(He grips FAGIN by the collar and shakes him as a dog shakes a rat.)*

              . . . Damnation to you. Why in hell's name couldn't you have kept him here among the rest, and made a sneaking, snivelling pickpocket of him at once?

FAGIN   *(With a shrug.)* Only hear him!

MONKS	Why, do you mean to say you couldn't have done it, if you had chosen? Haven't you done it with other boys, scores of times? If you had had patience for a twelvemonth, at most, couldn't you have got him convicted, and sent safely out of the kingdom; perhaps for life?
FAGIN	Whose turn would that have served, my dear? 80
MONKS	Mine.
FAGIN	But not mine. He would have become of use to me, my dear, but his hand was not in. I had nothing to frighten him with; which we always must have in the beginning, or we labour in vain. What could I do? Send him out with the Dodger, and Charley? We have enough of that at first, my dear; I trembled for us all. But do not worry. I got him back once, by means of the girl. I'll get him back again, or my name's not Fagin.
MONKS	You'd better, Fagin, or I'll break every bone in your nasty 90 body, d'you understand? There, take these papers, and hide 'em . . . *(He hands a small bundle of letters to FAGIN.)* . . . the only other proofs of that boy's identity now lie at the bottom of the river, and the old hag that took them from the mother is rotting in her coffin. His money is mine, Fagin, mine! But I won't feel safe until . . . *(He starts.)* . . . Fire this infernal den! What's that?
FAGIN	What? Where?
MONKS	Yonder! The shadow! I saw the shadow of a woman in a 100 cloak and bonnet, pass along the wainscot like a breath!
FAGIN	It's your fancy!
MONKS	I swear I saw it! It was bending forward when I saw it first. When I spoke, it darted away!
FAGIN	Besides ourselves, there's not a creature in the house except Toby and the boys; and they're safe enough. See here! . . .

(He draws MONKS forward to inspect the shadowy recesses at the head of the stairs.) . . . Come, we'll go to Bill's ken. He may be back there, by now. He'll know how to get Young Oliver back, if anyone does.

As long, my dear, as you're ready to make it worth his while.   110

(As soon as FAGIN and MONKS have gone, NANCY comes out from the dark corner in which she has been eaves dropping.)

NANCY   I'll go! I'll got to Chertsey! I'll warn them! I know where their crib is! No, no. That would be dangerous, to go there. I know what – I'll send 'em a message. I'll ask 'em to meet me somewhere – on London Bridge, say – on Sunday, between eleven and midnight. I'd rather that boy was dead, and out of harm's way, that be brought back to this place again, alive.   120

WRITING: In pairs, write the message which Nancy decides to send to the people in Chertsey. Are you surprised that she has decided to help Oliver?

DISCUSSION AND ARTWORK: Fagin is angry and nervous in this scene because he knows that Oliver is likely to give information to the police about him and other members of the gang.
   In small groups, compile the information on Fagin, Bill Sykes, Toby Crackit and The Artful Dodger that Oliver would be able to give to the police. Design wanted posters for the members of the gang.

WRITING: Write a 'Crimewatch'-style script outlining the crime at Chertsey, requesting information from the public and giving descriptions of the criminals involved. Practise delivering your script and be prepared to read it out to the class with plenty of eye contact and appropriate expression.

ACT 2 ❖ SCENE 7
BILL SIKES' KEN AT BETHNAL GREEN

OLIVER	But when the night came on which Nancy had arranged to meet the kind people who were giving me a home, she did not find it easy to keep the appointment.	1

(A clock strikes eleven. BILL SIKES comes in, with FAGIN.)

BILL SIKES An hour this side of midnight. Dark and 'eavy it is, too. A good night for business, this.

FAGIN Ah! What a pity, Bill my dear, that there's none quite ready to be done.

BILL SIKES	You're right for once. It's a pity, for I'm in the humour, too. We must make up for lost time when . . .	10

(NANCY comes in. She is wearing a bonnet.)

. . . Hallo! Nance! Where's the gal going to at this time of night?

NANCY Not far.

BILL SIKES What answer's that? Where are you going?

NANCY I say, not far.

BILL SIKES And I say where? Do you hear me?

NANCY I don't know where.

DILL SIKES Then I do. You're going nowhere. Sit down.

NANCY	I'm not well. I told you that before. I want a breath of air.	20

BILL SIKES Then put yer 'ead out of the winder.

NANCY There's not enough there. I want it in the street.

BILL SIKES Then you won't 'ave it . . .

(He locks the door, removes the key, and pulls the bonnet off her head.)

. . . There. Now stop quietly where yer are, will yer?

NANCY	It's not such a matter as a bonnet would keep me. What do you mean, Bill? Do you know what you are doing?
BILL SIKES	Know what I'm . . . Oh!

(He turns to FAGIN.)

30

. . . The wench is out of 'er senses, or she dursn't talk to me in that way.

NANCY	You'll drive me on to something desperate. Let me go, will you? . . . This minute! . . . This instant!
BILL SIKES	No!
NANCY	Tell him to let me go. Fagin. He had better. It'll be better for him. Do you hear me?
BILL SIKES	Hear you? Aye! And if I hear you for 'arf a minute longer I'll tear some of that screaming voice aht. Wot 'as come over you, you jade? Wot is it?

40

NANCY	Let me go! Bill, let me go; you don't know what you are doing. You don't indeed. For only one hour – do – do!
BILL SIKES	The girl's stark, raving made. Git up off the floor!
NANCY	Not till you lets me go . . . Not till you lets me go . . . Never . . . Never!

(She screams. BILL SIKES watches his opportunity, then he pinions her hands and drags her, struggling and wrestling by the

---

dursnt *an old form of 'wouldn't dare', ('dare not').*

jade *'worthless and deceitful woman'*

way, into an adjoining room. Her moans can be heard until BILL SIKES returns.)

BILL SIKES	That's settled 'er for a bit. I've strapped 'er to the bedpost. Wot a precious strange gal she is!	50
FAGIN	*(Thoughtfully.)* You may say that, Bill. You may say that.	
BILL SIKES	Wot did she tike it inter 'er 'ead to go out tonight for, do yer think? Wot does it mean?	
FAGIN	Obstinacy; woman's obstinacy, I suppose, my dear.	
BILL SIKES	I suppose it is. I thought I 'ad tamed 'er but she's as bad as ever . . .	

(There is an extra-loud scream from NANCY.)

. . . Come on, let's go and 'ave another look at 'er. Stuff 'er gob-'ole if she don't pipe dahn. 60

(BILL SIKES and FAGIN go out.)

DISCUSSION AND WRITING: In this scene, Bill treats Nancy like an animal. He ties her to the bedpost to prevent her leaving and says that he thought he had tamed her.

In a small group look back over the scenes in which Nancy appears, (Act 1, Scenes 4 & 6, Act 2, Scenes 4, 6 & 7). Talk over Nancy's feelings about Bill and the way in which he controls her.

Imagine that you are Nancy. Write a diary entry for each of the scenes mentioned above from her point of view. Make her feelings clear.

ROLE PLAY: In a group of three, prepare a television interview about relationships. One of you takes the part of the interviewer/presenter and introduces Mr Bumble and Nancy, and questions them about their relationships with Mrs Bumble and Bill Sikes.

ACT 2 ❖ SCENE 8
OUTSIDE AN ALE-HOUSE

OLIVER Fagin's suspicions were throughly aroused by Nancy's intransigence, and he determined to have her watched – if possible, by some one she could not conceivably recognise. He found a suitable candidate quite by chance, in the person of Noah Claypole, who had just arrived in London with Charlotte, and the contents of Mr Sowerberry's till.

(NOAH CLAYPOLE and CHARLOTTE, with a bundle each, and a glass and a half of ale, sit down at an outdoor table to continue a conversation.)

NOAH CLAYPOLE So I means ter be a gentleman. No more jolly old coffins, Charlotte, but a gentleman's life for me: and if yer like yer shall be a lady.

CHARLOTTE I should like that well enough, dear. But tills ain't to be emptied every day, and people to get clear off after it.

NOAH CLAYPOLE Tills be blowed! There's more things besides tills to be emptied.

CHARLOTTE What do you mean?

NOAH CLAYPOLE Pockets, women's ridicules, houses, mail-coaches, banks!

CHARLOTTE But you can't do all that, dear.

NOAH CLAYPOLE I shall look out to get into company with them as can. They'll be able to make us useful some way or another.

intransigeance *'stubborness'*

ridicules *Noah makes a mistake in his choice of word. He means* **reticules**, *meaning* **women's handbags.**

Why, you yourself are worth fifty women; I never see such a precious sly and deceitful creetur as yer can be when I lets yer.

CHARLOTTE Lor, how nice it is to hear you say so!

(She imprints a kiss on NOAH CLAYPOLE'S ugly face.)

NOAH CLAYPOLE There, that'll do: don't yer be too affectionate, in case I'm cross with yer.

(As NOAH CLAYPOLE disengages himself, FAGIN approaches the table.) 30

FAGIN A pleasant night, Sir, but cool for the time of year. From the country, I see, Sir?

NOAH CLAYPOLE How do yer see that?

FAGIN We have not so much dust as that in London.

(He points to the travellers' shoes, and then to their bundles.)

NOAH CLAYPOLE Yer a sharp feller. Ha! Ha! Only hear that, Charlotte.

FAGIN *(Sinking his voice to a confidential whisper.)* Why, one need be sharp in this town, my dear, and that's the truth . . . The . . .

(He taps NOAH CLAYPOLE'S glass.) 40

. . . The price of porter!

NOAH CLAYPOLE Good stuff that.

FAGIN Dear! Very dear! A man need be always emptying a till, or a pocket, or a woman's reticule, or a house, or a mail-coach, or a bank, if he drinks it regularly . . .

porter *a kind of beer.*

(*NOAH CLAYPOLE looks at him with a countenance of ashy paleness and excessive terror.*)

. . . Don't mind me, my dear! Ha! Ha! It was lucky it was only me that heard you by chance. It was very lucky it was only me.

5(

NOAH CLAYPOLE I didn't take it. It was all her doing. Yer've got it now, Charlotte, yer know yer have.

FAGIN No matter who's got it, or who did it, my dear . . .

(*He shoots a hawk-like glance at CHARLOTTE, and then at the two bundles.*)

. . . I'm that way inclined myself, and I like you for it. In fact, I wouldn't mind putting you in the way of a little bit of business where your talents could be usefully employed . . .

(*He leans over the table.*)

6

. . . I would like you to do a piece of work for me that needs great care and caution.

NOAH CLAYPOLE I say! Don't yer go shoving me into danger, or sending me near any of them police offices. That don't suit me, that don't; and so I tell yer.

FAGIN There's not the smallest danger in it . . . not the very smallest. It's only to dodge a woman.

NOAH CLAYPOLE An old woman?

FAGIN A young one.

NOAH CLAYPOLE I can do that pretty well, I know. I was a regular cunning sneak when I was at school. What am I to dodge her for?

7

dodge *thieves' slang for 'follow', 'keep an eye on and inform against'.*

	Not to . . .
FAGIN	Not to do anything, but to tell me where she goes, who she sees, and, if possible, what she says; to remember the street, if it is a street, or the house, if it is a house; and to bring me back all the information you can.
NOAH CLAYPOLE	What'll yer give me?
FAGIN	If you do it well, a pound, my dear. One pound! And that's what I never gave yet for any job of work where there wasn't valuable consideration to be gained.
NOAH CLAYPOLE	Who is she?
FAGIN	One of my . . . friends.
NOAH CLAYPOLE	Oh Lor! Yer doubtful of her, are yer?
FAGIN	She has found out some new friends, my dear, and I must know who they are.
NOAH CLAYPOLE	I see. Just to have the pleasure of knowing them, if they're respectable people, eh? Ha! Ha! Ha! I'm yer man.
FAGIN	I knew you would be.
NOAH CLAYPOLE	Of course, of course, Where is she? Where am I to wait for her? Where am I to go?
FAGIN	All that, my dear, you shall hear from me. I'll point her out at the proper time. Just step this way, will you, and leave the rest to me?

80

90

IMPROVISATION AND WRITING: You already know Noah to be a mean and cowardly bully so it is not surprising that he has also turned thief.

In groups of four improvise, practise and script two extra short scenes:

1 Noah and Charlotte planning to steal the contents of Mr Sowerberry's till.
2 Mr and Mrs Sowerberry's discovery of and reaction to the crime.

ACT 2 ❖ SCENE 9
AT FAGIN'S

(It is nearly two hours before daybreak, and FAGIN sits watching in his lair. At first it is too dark for us to see him. Then, as four o'clock strikes, we can dimly perceive him as he sits crouched over his cold hearth, wrapped in an old torn coverlet.

Stretched on a mattress on the floor we can see NOAH CLAYPOLE fast asleep. There is a gentle knock at the street door.)

FAGIN At last . . .

(He wipes his dry and fevered mouth.)

. . . At last!

(He goes to the door, and returns with BILL SIKES, who is muffled to the chin, and carrying a bundle.)

BILL SIKES There! . . .

(The robber lays the bundle on the table.)

. . . Take care of that, and do the most you can with it. It's been trouble enough to get: I thought I should have been here three hours ago . . .

(FAGIN locks the bundle away, without taking his eyes off BILL SIKES for an instant.)

. . . Wot now? Wot do you look at a man so for? . . .

(FAGIN raises his right hand, but his passion is so great that he has lost the power of speech.)

. . . Damme! He's gone mad. I must look to myself here.

FAGIN No, no . . . It's not . . . You're not the person, Bill. I've no . . . no fault to find with you.

BILL SIKES	Oh, you haven't, haven't you? . . .
	(He ostentatiously passes a pistol into a more convenient pocket.) 20
	. . . That's lucky for one of us. Which one that is, don't matter.
FAGIN	I've got that to tell you, Bill, will make you worse than me.
BILL SIKES	Aye? Tell away! Look sharp, or Nance will think I'm lost.
FAGIN	Lost! She has pretty well settled that in her own mind already.
BILL SIKES	*(Clutching FAGIN'S coat collar in his huge hand and shaking him soundly.)* Speak, will you! Open your mouth and say wot you've got to say in plain words. Out with it, you thundering old cur, out with it! 30
FAGIN	Suppose that lad that's lying there . . .
	(BILL SIKES turns to look at NOAH CLAYPOLE.)
BILL SIKES	Well?
FAGIN	Suppose that lad was to peach . . . to blow upon us all . . . first seeking out the right folks for the purpose, and then having a meeting with 'em in the street to paint our likenesses, describe every mark that they might know us by, and the crib where we might be most easily taken. Suppose he was to do all this, and besides to blow upon a plant we've all been in, more or less, of his own fancy; not 40 grabbed, trapped, tried, earwigged by the parson and brought to it on bread and water, but of his own fancy; to

---

ostentatiously *'in a deliberately showy way'* so that Fagin is bound to see.

to blow upon us all *'to inform against all of us'*

to blow upon a plant *'to tell the police of an intended robbery'*

earwigged by the parson *persuaded in secret by the prison chaplain to inform against others involved in the crime.*

please his own taste; stealing out at nights to find those most interested against us, and peaching to them. Do you hear me? . . .

(His eyes flash with rage.)

. . . Suppose he did all this, what then?

BILL SIKES   What then, by Gar! If he was left alive till I came, I'd grind his skull under the iron heel of my boot into as many grains as there are hairs upon his head.

FAGIN   What if I did it? I, that know so much, and could hang so many besides myself!

BILL SIKES   I'd do something in the jail that 'ud get me put in irons; and if I was tried along with you, I'd fall upon you with them in the open court, and I'd beat out your brains afore the people. I should have such strength . . .

(He poises his brawny arm.)

. . . that I could smash your head as if a loaded wagon had gone over it.

FAGIN   You would?

BILL SIKES   Would I? Try me!

FAGIN   If it was Charley, or The Dodger, or Crackit, or . . .

BILL SIKES   *(Impatiently.)* I don't care who. Whoever it was, I'd serve them the same.

(Motioning BILL SIKES to be silent, FAGIN stoops over the bed on the floor and shakes NOAH CLAYPOLE, to rouse him.)

I could smash your head as if a loaded wagon had gone over it *Bill gives an accurate account of his own brutality.*

If it was Charley, or The Dodger, or Crackit, or . . . *Fagin deliberately leaves an unspoken name hanging in the air. He cleverly manipulates Bill's brutal anger in this scene.*

FAGIN	Poor lad! He's tired . . . tired with watching for her, Bill.
BILL SIKES	*(Drawing back.)* Wot d'ye mean?
	(FAGIN bends over NOAH CLAYPOLE again, and hauls him into a sitting posture. NOAH rubs his eyes, yawns, and looks sleepily about him.) 70
FAGIN	*(To NOAH CLAYPOLE.)* Tell me that again . . .
	(He points to BILL SIKES.)
	. . . Once again, just for him to hear.
NOAH CLAYPOLE	Tell yer what?
FAGIN	That about – NANCY . . .
	(He clutches SIKES by the wrist as if to prevent him leaving the house before he has heard enough.)
	. . . You followed her?
NOAH CLAYPOLE	Yes. 80
FAGIN	To London Bridge?
NOAH CLAYPOLE	Yes.
FAGIN	Where she met two people?
NOAH CLAYPOLE	So she did.
FAGIN	A gentleman and a lady? . . .
	(NOAH CLAYPOLE nods.)
	. . . Who asked her to give up all her pals . . . and to tell where we do meet . . . and where it can best be watched from . . . and what time the people go there, which she did. She did all this. She told it all, every word, without a threat, 90 without a murmur – she did – did she not?
NOAH CLAYPOLE	That's right . . . That's just what it was!
FAGIN	What did they say, about last Sunday?

107

NOAH CLAYPOLE	About last Sunday? Why, I told yer that before.
FAGIN	Again. Tell it again!
NOAH CLAYPOLE	They asked her why she didn't come last Sunday, as she promised. She said she couldn't.
FAGIN	Why – Why? Tell him that.
NOAH CLAYPOLE	Because she was forcibly kept home by Bill, the man she was telling them of.
BILL SIKES	Hell's fire! . . . Let me go!

(He breaks fiercely from FAGIN'S grasp and rushes toward the door.)

FAGIN	Bill! Bill! A word! Only a word!
BILL SIKES	Let me out! Don't speak to me; it's not safe. Let me out, I say!
FAGIN	Hear me speak a word. You won't be . . . You won't be . . . too . . . violent, Bill? I mean, not too violent for safety. Be crafty, Bill, and not too bold.

(BILL SIKES makes no reply, but rushes into the silent streets.)

WRITING: Add any new terms of thieves' slang together with explanations to the list you began after reading Act 1, Scene 4 and added to after reading Act 2, Scene 4.

DISCUSSION: At the end of this scene, Fagin pleads with Bill not to be 'too violent for safety'.
   In pairs, read back through the parts of Bill and Fagin. Discuss and write down the way in which Fagin manipulates Bill into dealing violently with Nancy.

For example:
1 When Fagin says, 'I've no fault to find with you', he is suggesting that he has fault to find with someone else.

ACT 2 ❖ SCENE 10
BILL SIKES' KEN

OLIVER TWIST	Without one pause, or moment's consideration; without turning his head to the right or left, or raising his eyes to the sky, or lowering them to the ground, but looking before him with savage resolution the robber held on his headlong course, nor muttered a word, nor relaxed a muscle, until he reached his own door. He opened it, softly, with a key; strode lightly up the stairs; entered his own room; double-locked the door, and, having lifted a heavy table against it, approached the bed.	1
BILL SIKES	*(Rousing NANCY, who is lying there half-dressed.)* Get up!	10
NANCY	It is you, Bill?	
BILL SIKES	It is. Get up . . . *(He extinguishes the candle. NANCY rises to undraw the curtain, but he thrusts his hand before her.)* . . . Let it be. There's light enough for wot I've got to do.	
NANCY	Bill! Why do you look like that at me? . . . *(He looks at her for a few seconds, with dilated nostrils and heaving breast; then, grasping her by the head and throat he drags her into the middle of the room, and, looking once towards the door, places his heavy hand upon her mouth.)* . . . Bill! Bill! I . . . I won't scream or cry . . . not once . . . hear me . . . speak to me . . . tell me what I have done!	20
BILL SIKES	You know, you she-devil! . . . You were watched tonight; every word you said was heard.	
NANCY	Then spare my life, for the love of Heaven, as I spared yours. Bill! Dear Bill! You cannot have the heart to kill me. Oh, think of all I have given up, only this one night, for you. You shall have time to think, and save yourself this	

crime; I will not loose my hold, you cannot throw me off. Bill, Bill, for dear God's sake, for your own, for mine, stop before you spill my blood! I have been true to you, upon my guilty soul I have! . . .

(He struggles violently to release his arms.)

. . . Bill! The gentleman, and that dear lady, told me tonight of a home in some foreign country where I could end my days in solitude and peace. Let me see them again, and beg them on my knees, to show the same mercy and goodness to you; and let us both leave this dreadful place, and far apart lead better lives, and forget how we have lived, except in prayers, and never see each other more. It is never too late to repent. They told me so . . . I feel it now . . . but we must have time . . . a little, little time!

(The housebreaker frees one arm, and grasps his pistol. The certainty of immediate detection, if he fires, flashes across his mind even in the midst of his fury; and he beats twice, with all the force he can summon, upon the upturned face that almost touches his own.)

OLIVER   Nancy staggered and fell, nearly blinded with the blood that rained down from a deep gash in her forehead. Then she raised herself with difficulty upon her knees.

NANCY   Mercy, Lord, have mercy . . .

OLIVER   It was a ghastly figure to look upon. The murderer staggered backward to the wall, and shutting out the sight with his hand seized a heavy club and struck her down.

EXPLORING LANGUAGE: Nancy's language in this scene shows her change of heart. Even though she makes some references to violence, most of her words are connected to God and to peace.

In pairs list some of the phrases in this scene and the last under the following headings:

	Violence	God and Peace
E. g.	Spill my blood	for the love of heaven

ACT 2 ❖ SCENE 11
A STREET CORNER

A NEWSBOY   Piper! Piper! Murder in Beffnal Green! Murder in Beffnal   1
Green! Piper! Piper! . . .

(A customer approaches.)

. . . Piper, Sir? Thank you, Sir? Yes, Sir, foul murder in
Beffnal Green, Sir. Woman found battered to death, Sir . . .

(He calls out again, as the customer moves away.)

. . . Piper! Piper! Big 'unt fer murderer! Big 'unt fer
murderer! Piper! Piper! . . .

(Another customer approaches.)

. . . Piper, Sir? Thank you, Sir. Yes, Sir. 'Arf the country's   10
'unting fer 'im, Sir . . .

(He calls out again, as the customer moves away.)

. . . Piper! Piper! Reward offered in murder 'unt! Reward
offered in murder 'unt! Piper! Piper! . . .

(A third customer approaches.)

. . . Piper, Sir? Thank you, Sir, Yussir, they think they've got
'im, Sir. In sarth-east Lunnon, Sir, dahn by the river, Sir. Got
dogs arter 'im, an 'all. Wouldn't like to be 'im, nah. 'Ere,
blow me pipers! I'm goinga see the fun!

WRITING: Plan and write a sensational, front page newspaper article
about the murder in Bethnal Green.

ACT 2 ❖ SCENE 12
THE KEN ON JACOB'S ISLAND

(A gloomy attic, in a ruinous house on desolate island. TOBY CRACKIT is crouching by the window. He is accompanied by two of FAGIN'S confederates, KAGS and CHITLING.)

TOBY CRACKIT   When was Fagin took, then?

CHITLING   Just at dinner-time . . . two o'clock this arternoon. Charley and I made our lucky up the wash'us chimney, and Claypole got into the empty water-butt, 'ead downwards, but 'is legs was so precious long that they stuck out at the top, and so they took 'im too.

TOBY CRACKIT   Wot's come of young Bates?

CHITLING   'E 'ung abaht, so as not to come over 'ere afore dark, but 'e'll be 'ere soon. There's nowhere else to go to, now. All the other kens is filled with traps.

TOBY CRACKIT   *(Biting his lips.)* This is a smash! There's more than one will go with this.

KAGS   The sessions is on. If they gets the inquest over, and that Claypole turns King's Evidence: as of course 'e will, from

The ken on Jacob's Island *the secret hiding place at Jacob's Island or Folly Ditch in Southwark; it is a real place – a notorious 19th Century slum area where thieves and prostitutes lived.*

made our lucky *'managed to escape' (a shortened form of made a lucky escape).*

smash *'catastrophe' a cutting blow.*

sessions *'sittings of courts of criminal justice'*

turns King's Evidence *gives evidence to the police in the hope of a lighter sentence.*

what 'e's said already: they can prove Fagin an accessory before the fact, and get the trial on Friday, and he'll swing in six days from this, by God.

CHITLING   You should 'ave 'eard the people groan. The officers fought like devils, or they'd 'ave torn 'im away. 'E was dahn once, but they made a ring round him, and fought their way   20
along. You should have seen 'ow 'e looked abaht 'im, all muddy and bleeding, and clung . . .

(He stops speaking, and listens to a distant pattering noise.)

. . . What's that? . . .

(The three men peep through the window to the courtyard below.)

. . . It's Sikes's dog!

TOBY CRACKIT   What's the meaning of this? 'E can't be coming 'ere! By Gar, we'll be took if 'e does.

CHITLING   The cur looks 'arf blind.

KAGS   And lame.   30

CHITLING   'E must 'ave come a long way.

TOBY CRACKIT   Where can 'e 'ave come from? I reckon 'e's been to the other kens and found 'em full of strangers. That's why 'e's come on 'ere. But 'ow come 'e's 'ere without the other?

CHITLING   The man can't 'ave made away with 'issell, do you think?

KAGS   Nah. If 'e 'ad, the dog 'ud 'ave wanted ter stay wiv 'im. No. I think 'e's got out of the country and left the dog be'ind. 'E must 'ave given the brute the slip some'ow, or 'e wouldn't . . .

an accessory before the fact *This is a legal term meaning* an accomplice *(in the murder of Nancy).*

(There is a hurried knocking at the door below. All three men show their alarm in different ways.)   4(

. . . 'Tis Young Bates!

(The knocking comes again.)

TOBY CRACKIT   No, it's not 'im. Young Bates 'ud never knock like that. It's . . . it's the other. We must let 'im in.

CHITLING   Ain't there any 'elp fer it?

TOBY CRACKIT   None. 'E must come in.

(TOBY CRACKIT goes out. When he returns, he is followed by a man with the lower part of his face buried in a handkerchief. Blanched face, sunken eyes, hollow cheeks, beard of three days'   5(
growth, wasted flesh – it is the very ghost of BILL SIKES. SIKES looks from one to another in silence. If an eye is furtively raised and meets his, it is instantly averted.)

BILL SIKES   *(At last.)* I've 'eard that Fagin's took. Is it true, or a lie?

TOBY CRACKIT   True.

(The men are silent again.)

BILL SIKES   Damn you all! Have you nothing to say to me? . . .

(There is an uneasy movement, but nobody speaks.)

. . . You that keep this house . . .

(He turns his face to TOBY CRACKIT.)   6(

. . . Do you mean to sell me, or to let me lie here till this hunt is over?

TOBY CRACKIT   *(After some hesitation.)* You may stop 'ere if yer think it safe.

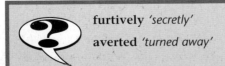

furtively *'secretly'*
averted *'turned away'*

BILL SIKES	Is . . . it . . . the body . . . is it buried? . . .

(The men shake their heads.)

. . . Why isn't it? Wot do they keep such ugly things above the ground for? . . .

(There is a knock at the door.)

. . . Who's that knocking?

(TOBY CRACKIT goes to see, and returns with CHARLEY BATES.) 70

CHARLEY BATES	*(Seeing BILL SIKES, and drawing back.)* Toby! Why didn't yer tell me this, downstairs? . . .

(BILL SIKES advances, as if he wishes to shake hands with the boy.)

. . . Let me go!

BILL SIKES	Charley! Don't yer . . . Don't yer know me?
CHARLEY BATES	Don't come nearer me! You monster! . . .

(The murderer and the boy look at each other. Then BILL SIKES'S eyes sink gradually to the ground.) 80

. . . Witness you three – I'm not afraid of 'im . . . If they come here after 'im, I'll give 'im up, I will. I tell you out at once. 'E may kill me fer it if 'e likes, or if 'e dares, but if I am 'ere I'll give 'im up . . . Murder! 'Elp! . . .

(He dashes to the window.)

. . . Murder! 'Elp! If there's the pluck of a man among you three, you'll 'elp me. Murder! 'Elp! Down wiv 'im! . . .

(CHARLEY BATES flings himself at BILL SIKES. The two roll on the ground in a desperate struggle, the boy never ceasing to call for help with all his might. BILL SIKES has YOUNG BATES down, with his knee on the boy's throat, when TOBY CRACKIT pulls him back with a look of alarm and points to the window. 90

There are lights gleaming below, voices in loud and earnest conversation, the tramp of hurried footsteps crossing the nearest wooden bridge. Then comes a loud knocking at the door.)

. . . 'Elp! 'E's 'ere! 'E's 'ere! Break down the door!

VOICES OUTSIDE   In the King's name!

CHARLEY BATES   Break down the door! They'll never open it . . . Break down the door!

(Strokes, thick and heavy, rattle upon the door and window shutters.)   10

BILL SIKES   That door! Quick! *(He seizes CHARLEY BATES, and drags him out, kicking and struggling. Then he returns, having bolted the boy away.)*

. . . Is the downstairs door fast?

TOBY CRACKIT   Double-locked and chained.

BILL SIKES   The panels . . . Are they strong?

TOBY CRACKIT   Lined with sheet-iron.

BILL SIKES   And the winders, too?

TOBY CRACKIT   Yus, and the winders.   12

BILL SIKES   *(Going to the window and menacing the crowd.)* Do yer worst! I'll cheat yer yet! . . .

(There are cries from the infuriated throng outside: 'Set the house on fire!' 'Shoot him!' 'Twenty guineas to the man who brings a ladder!')

. . . Give me a rope. A long rope. They're all in front. I may drop inter Folly Ditch, and clear off that way. Give me a rope, or I shall do three more murders.

(TOBY CRACKIT produces a long, strong cord. BILL SIKES takes it, and goes out to a window at the back of the house.)   13

THE CROWD   He's out on the roof! He's out at the back! Come on!

TOBY CRACKIT	'E's gone out of that little winder on to the roof. Come 'ere. Crouch dahn. You can see 'im through this . . .

(The three men crouch down.)

. . . Look! 'E's tying a noose in the rope. 'E's going to tie the other end rahnd the chimney stack, I tell yer.

CHITLING	No, 'e ain't.

TOBY CRACKIT	What's 'e going to tie it rahnd, then? There you are! What did I tell yer? 'E 'as. Nah, 'e's goin' ter let hisself dahn . . .

(Cries of 'Keep back!' 'He's going to jump for it!')   140

. . . 'E's slipped! Chrisalmighty, 'e's slipped!

(There is an unearthly screech from outside as BILL SIKES falls thirty-five feet.)

. . . 'E's 'anged 'isself! Oh, Gor, the poor creetur! 'E's gone and 'anged 'isself.

CHITLING	What 'ad we better do now?

TOBY CRACKIT	We'd better scarper quick. We can git away, mebbe, if we makes a dash while they're a-thinking of cutting 'im dahn. C'mon. 'Urry.

(The three men make off, leaving CHARLEY BATES to call to the   150
people to let him out.)

WRITING AND ROLEPLAY: In pairs imagine that you are part of a television news team that has been sent to cover the exciting police siege of the ken on Jacob's Island. Together plan and write a live broadcast. Start with a brief description of the ken. Give the information that Sikes's dog and a man believed to be Sikes arrived a short while earlier and that sounds of a violent struggle have been heard within. Report the remaining action on the roof as though it is happening as you speak. Practise delivering the broadcast with appropriate pace and expression and be prepared to deliver it to the whole class.

WRITING: Write a newspaper article on the events of this scene, covering the arrest of Fagin, the flight of Sikes and his violent end on Jacob's Island.

ACT 2 ❖ SCENE 13
A PRIVATE ROOM IN A HOTEL NEAR THE WORKHOUSE

(MR BROWNLOW leads two sturdy men into the room. These men are escorting MONKS, who has been brought there under duress. At the rear of the procession we see MR GRIMWIG and YOUNG OLIVER.)

MR BROWNLOW   He knows the alternative. If he hesitates, or moves a finger but as you bid him, drag him into the street, call for the aid of the police, and impeach him as a felon in my name.

MONKS   How dare you do this to me? By what authority am I kidnapped in the street and brought here by these dogs?

MR BROWNLOW   By mine. Those persons are indemnified by me. If you complain of being deprived of your liberty, throw yourself for protection on the law. I will appeal to the law, too; but when you have gone too far to recede, do not sue to me for leniency, for then the power will have passed into other hands . . .

(MONKS hesitates.)

. . . You will decide quickly if you wish me to prefer my charges publicly, and consign you to dire punishment. If

duress *'force'*

impeach him as a felon *'accuse him of a serious crime'*

indemnified by me . . . *freed from blame and protected against legal responsibility because acting under Mr Brownlow's orders.*

do not sue to me for leniency *'do not apply to me for a lighter punishment'* Mr Brownlow uses a series of legal terms here which suggest the force of his accusations and that he has right on his side.

not, if you appeal to my forbearance, and the mercy of those you have deeply injured, seat yourself, without a word, in that chair. It has waited for you for long enough . . .

(MONKS mutters some unintelligible words.)

. . . You will be prompt. A word from me, and the alternative has gone for ever . . .   20

(Still MONKS hesitates.)

. . . I have not the inclination to parley, and as I advocate the dearest interests of others, I have not the right.

MONKS	Is there . . . is there . . . no middle course?
MR BROWNLOW	None . . .

(MONKS reads in MR BROWNLOW'S countenance nothing but severity and determination, so he shrugs his shoulders and sits down. MR BROWNLOW turns to the attendants.)

. . . Please wait outside, and come if I ring.   30

(The attendants go out.)

MONKS	This is pretty treatment, Sir, from my father's oldest friend.
MR BROWNLOW	It is a painful task, but these declarations which have been made in London before many gentlemen must be in substance repeated here.
MONKS	Go on. Quick. I have almost done enough, I think. Don't keep me here.
MR BROWNLOW	This child . . .

forbearance *'patience and tolerance'*

advocate *Mr Brownlow is putting forward the rights of other people.*

(He draws YOUNG OLIVER to him, and lays his hand upon his head.)   40

... Whom I intend to adopt herewith as my own son, is your half brother, the illegitimate son of your father, my dear friend Edwin Leeford, by poor young Agnes Fleming, who died in giving him birth.

MONKS   Must I be forced to listen to this?

MR BROWNLOW   When your father died, so suddenly and tragically, he left on his desk two papers. One was a letter to this Agnes. The second was his will.

MONKS   I have nothing to disclose. Talk on, if you must.

MR BROWNLOW   Your mother did what she considered to be her duty. She   50
destroyed the will, leaving the secret, and the gain, to you at her own death. It contained a reference to some child likely to be the result of his sad connection. This child was accidentally encountered by you, and your suspicions were first awakened by his resemblance to his father. You repaired to the place of his birth. There existed proofs – proofs long suppressed – of his birth and parentage. Those proofs were destroyed by you, and now, in your own words to your accomplice Fagin, 'the only proofs of the boy's identity lie at the bottom of the river, and the old hag that   60
received them from the mother is rotting in her coffin.' Unworthy son, coward, liar – you, who hold your councils with thieves and murderers in dark rooms at night – you, Edward Leeford, do you still brave me?

MONKS   No! No! No!

MR BROWNLOW   Then you will tell us, no doubt, what happened to Agnes' locket, and ring?

MONKS   I bought them from a vile old woman at the workhouse, who stole them from the nurse, who stole them from the corpse. You know what became of them.   70

(MR BROWNLOW nods to MR GRIMWIG, who disappears with great alacrity, and shortly returns pushing in MRS BUMBLE, and dragging her unwilling consort after him.)

MR BUMBLE	Do my hi's deceive me? Or is that little Oliver? Oh, O–li–ver, if you know'd how I've been a-grieving for you –
MRS BUMBLE	Hold your tongue, fool.
MR GRIMWIG	*(Tartly.)* Come, Sir. Suppress your feelings.
MR BUMBLE	I will do my endeavours, Sir . . .

(He turns to MR BROWNLOW.)

. . . How do you do, Sir? I hope you are very well?   80

MR BROWNLOW	*(Pointing to MONKS.)* Do you know that person?
MRS BUMBLE	No.
MR BROWNLOW	*(To MR BUMBLE.)* Perhaps you don't?
MR BUMBLE	I never saw him in all my life.
MR BROWNLOW	Nor sold him anything, perhaps?
MRS BUMBLE	No.
MR BROWNLOW	You never had, perhaps a certain gold locket and ring?
MRS BUMBLE	Certainly not! Why are we brought here to answer such nonsense as this?

*(Again MR BROWNLOW nods to MR GRIMWIG. This time,   90
MR GRIMWIG produces the two workhouse females who
watched over OLD SALLY'S deathbed.)*

THE FEMALE PAUPER	You sent us away, the night Old Sally died, but our ears is long, old as we be.
THE OLD WOMAN	*(Looking round, and wagging her toothless jaws.)* Ay, ay!
THE FEMALE PAUPER	We heard her try to tell you what she'd done, and saw you take a paper from her hand, and watched you, too, the next day, to the pawnbroker's shop.

THE OLD WOMAN	Yes, and it was a locket and gold ring. We saw it given you. We were by. Oh! We were by.

100

MR GRIMWIG	(To MRS BUMBLE, with a motion towards the door.) Would you like to see the pawnbroker himself?
MRS BUMBLE	No. If he . . .

(She points to MONKS.)

. . . has been coward enough to confess, as I see he has, I have nothing more to say. I did sell them. What of that?

MR BROWNLOW	Nothing. Except that it remains for us to take care that neither of you is employed in a situation of trust again. You may leave the room.
MR BUMBLE	(Looking round with great ruefulness as MR GRIMWIG disappears with the three women.) I hope that this unfortunate little circumstance will not deprive me of my porochial office?

110

MR BROWNLOW	Indeed it will. You may make up your mind to that, and think yourself well off besides.
MR BUMBLE	It was all Mrs Bumble. She would do it.
MR BROWNLOW	That is no excuse. You were a party to the destruction of these trinkets, and indeed are the more guilty of the two, in the eye of the law, for the law supposes that your wife acts under your direction.

120

MR BUMBLE	(Squeezing his hat.) If the law supposes that, the law is a hass . . . the law is a hidiot. If that's the eye of the law, the law is a bachelor; and the worst I wish the law is, that his eye may be opened by experience – by experience.

(MR BUMBLE fixes his hat on very tight, and goes out.)

MR BROWNLOW	And now, Oliver my son, we have one more duty to perform before we can say that justice has truly been carried out. It will not be a pleasant one, but . . .

(MR GRIMWIG returns, and signals to MR BROWNLOW.)

. . . My boy, our carriage awaits.   130

(MR BROWNLOW leads OLIVER affectionately out. The sturdy men, bidden by MR GRIMWIG, remove MONKS.)

ruefulness *mournful repentance.*

It was all Mrs Bumble. She would do it *Mr Bumble is very quick to lay all the blame on Mrs Bumble in much the same way that Noah tried to blame Charlotte in Act 2, Scene 8*

the law is a bachelor *This very famous line shows how Mr Bumble's understanding has grown through the experience of marriage. Only a bachelor could believe that a man might be in charge of a woman with the violent determination of Mrs Bumble.*

WRITING: The story of the novel of *Oliver Twist* is told in the third person by Charles Dickens. In this play, the adult Oliver sometimes tells part of the story in the first person. E.g. at the beginning of the play he says 'Have you ever been hungry? . . . *I've* been like that for weeks and months at a time. You see, I was born at a charity Workhouse . . .'

Young Oliver is a silent witness to all that is said and done in Scene 13. Think carefully about his feelings.

Write an addition to this scene in the form of a speech for Oliver, the young man, looking back at his childhood. You might begin with: 'At last I had found out the truth about my mother . . .'

Write a first-person diary extract covering two separate incidents in the play from Oliver's viewpoint. Give each extract a different setting: at the Workhouse, at Fagin's or at Mr Brownlow's. Try to cover Oliver's feelings as well as what happens. Include quotations from the play.

ACT 2 ❖ SCENE 14
THE CONDEMNED CELL AT NEWGATE

(MR BROWNLOW presents an order of admission to the prisoner. He is accompanied by YOUNG OLIVER.)

THE CHIEF WARDEN Is the young gentleman to come too, Sir? It's not a sight for children, Sir.

MR BROWNLOW It is not indeed, my friend; but my business with this man is intimately connected with him; and as this child has seen him in the full career of his success and villainy, I think it as well – even at the cost of some pain and fear – that he should see him now.

(THE CHIEF WARDER touches his hat and leads the visitors towards the cells.)

THE CHIEF WARDEN *(Pausing on the way.)* This is the place he will pass through, Sir, when the clock strikes eight. If you step this way, you can see the door he goes out at.

MR BROWNLOW And what is that noise?

THE CHIEF WARDEN They're just a-putting the finishing touches to the scaffold, Sir. The crowd's been growing since midnight.

(They pass into the Condemned Cell. FAGIN is seated on his bed, rocking himself from side to side, with a countenance more like that of a snared beast than the face of a man.)

FAGIN *(Mumbling to himself.)* Good boy, Charley . . . Well done . . . Oliver, too, ha! ha! ha! Oliver, too; . . . quite the gentleman now . . . quite the . . . take that boy away to bed . . . Take him away! . . . Do you hear me, some of you?

THE CHIEF WARDEN Fagin!

FAGIN That's me! An old man, my Lord; a very old, old man.

THE CHIEF WARDEN	Here . . . Here's somebody wants to see you, to ask you some questions, I suppose. Fagin! Fagin! Are you a man?
FAGIN	*(Looking up with a face retaining no human expression but rage and terror.)* I shan't be one long. Strike them all dead! What right have they to butcher me? . . .
	(He catches sight of YOUNG OLIVER and MR BROWNLOW and shrinks to the furthest corner of the seat.) 30
	. . . What do you want? Ah! Ah! What do you want?
THE CHIEF WARDEN	*(Holding FAGIN down.)* Steady! . . . *(He turns to MR BROWNLOW.)*
	. . . Now, Sir, tell him what you want. Quick, if you please, for he grows worse as the time comes closer.
MR BROWNLOW	*(Advancing.)* You have some papers, which were placed in your hands, for better security, by a man called Monks.
FAGIN	It's a lie together. I haven't one – not one.
MR BROWNLOW	For the love of Goodness, do not say that now, upon the very verge of death; but tell me where they are. You know that Sikes is dead; that Monks has confessed; that there is no hope of any further gain. Where are those papers? 40
FAGIN	*(Beckoning to YOUNG OLIVER.)* Oliver! Here, here! Let me whisper to you.
YOUNG OLIVER	*(Relinquishing MR BROWNLOW'S hand.)* I am not afraid.
FAGIN	*(Drawing YOUNG OLIVER towards him.)* The papers are in a canvas bag, in a hole a little way up the chimney in the top front-room. I want to talk to you, my dear. I want to talk to you. 50

An old man, my lord; a very old, old man *The repetition of old and the simplicity of this statement introduces a note of pity for Fagin as he waits in the condemned cell.*

YOUNG OLIVER	Yes, yes. Let me say a prayer. Do! Let me say one prayer. Say only one, upon your knees with me, and we will talk till morning.
FAGIN	*(Pushing YOUNG OLIVER before him towards the door.)* Outside, outside. Say I've gone to sleep – they'll believe you. You can get me out, if you take me so. Now then, now then!
YOUNG OLIVER	Oh, God forgive this wretched man!
FAGIN	That's right, that's right. That'll help us on. This door first. If I shake and tremble, as we pass the gallows, don't you mind, but hurry on. Now, now, now!
THE CHIEF WARDEN	Have you nothing else to ask him, Sir?
MR BROWNLOW	No other question. If I hoped we could recall him to a sense of his position . . .
THE CHIEF WARDEN	*(Shaking his head.)* Nothing will do that, Sir. You had better leave him.
	(WARDERS appear.)
FAGIN	Press on. Press on. Softly, but not too slow. Faster! Faster!
	(The WARDERS disengage YOUNG OLIVER from FAGIN'S grasp. FAGIN sends up cry after cry as MR BROWNLOW leads YOUNG OLIVER from the cell. Then Newgate Bell starts to toll, and the WARDERS bow their heads. On the eighth stroke, THE HANGMAN and his assistants enter the cell. They pinion FAGIN, and take him out to the scaffold.)

DISCUSSION AND WRITING: In a group, look back through he evidence you have compiled on the character of Fagin and decide whether or not Fagin deserves to be executed.

Write a short speech either for or against the hanging of Fagin. Use evidence from the play and your own view of capital punishment. Practise your speech.

LOOKING BACK AT THE PLAY

1   ARTWORK: A COMIC STRIP

Almost all the main events of the novel of *Oliver Twist* are included in this dramascript. One strand of the story is left out: it concerns the people living in the house that Sikes and Toby Crackit try to burgle in Chertsey.

Working in a small group select twelve individual incidents or clips from the play which tell the whole story of *Oliver Twist*. Design a comic strip of the story, using each clip as a frame. At least one person in the group should be prepared to work on the illustrations. Plan in rough first, deciding on captions and thought bubbles.

2   DISCUSSION: GOOD AND BAD CHARACTERS

Some people are critical of the characters in the novel *Oliver Twist*. In real life, people are rarely wholly good or bad but many of the characters in this novel seem to be either perfect or totally evil. What do you think?

In a small group, work through the character list at the front of the play and list each character under one of the following headings:

Good	Evil	Partly good	Partly evil

Collect evidence for your decisions. For example, Mr Brownlow might be placed under the heading *Good*, the evidence being: he is very kind and caring to Oliver; he takes Oliver into his house when he knows nothing about him except that he was in the company of thieves and pickpockets; he never loses his trust in Oliver even when the boy disappears with some of his money and books and he works with determination to find the truth about Oliver's identity. There are some obvious candidates for the wholly bad list but it is more tricky to identify those who are partly good and partly bad. You will need contradictory evidence here to prove your point. Share your findings with the rest of the class.

3   WRITING: INTERESTING CHARACTERS

Wilkie Collins, a famous writer and friend of Dickens' claimed that Nancy was the only interesting character in *Oliver Twist*.

Choose the two characters you find most interesting in the play and write an account of each. Check through the activities you did as you worked through the play for information and evidence. You should include details of personal appearance and position; the kind of language used; some actual quotations; some reference to actions and intentions and an explanation of what makes each character interesting.

4 WRITING AND DISCUSSION: POOR CHILDREN

Perhaps because Dickens had been poor himself, he was concerned about the welfare of poor people throughout his life. He was also concerned about the numbers of children drawn into lives of crime in London. He wrote *Oliver Twist* with these interests and the following purposes in mind:

1 To mount an attack on the New Poor Law which forced the poor to live in the workhouse where families were separated and diet was very close to starvation level.
2 To bring to public attention the existence of slum-like areas of London in which prostitution and violent crime flourished and into which poor children were sucked.

Working in a small group imagine that you are a team of researchers for a documentary television programme on the plight of poor children in the 1830s and 40s. You have been asked to provide information under the following headings:

1 Children and the workhouse
2 Children in apprenticeships
3 Children involved in crime.

Gather your information from those scenes set in the workhouse, at Fagin's and at Mr Sowerberry's. Make notes and report your findings orally.

5 WRITING AND ROLEPLAY: A TELEVISION DOCUMENTARY

Plan and practise a six or seven minute insert into a television documentary on the subjects you researched in the last activity. Decide on roles within the group: a presenter/interviewer and researcher/speakers on each topic. Be prepared to speak with minimal use of notes and direct eye contact.

6 WRITING: A HISTORY TEXTBOOK

Write three short inserts for a textbook on social history of the 1830s and 40s under the three headings given above. Use detail given in the play and try to be clear and formal.

7 WRITING: A GLOSSARY OF THIEVES' SLANG.

When Dickens wrote *Oliver Twist,* he was living near a notoriously crime-ridden area of London called Saffron Hill. He was a sharp social observer and swiftly familiarised himself with the special terminology of the criminal community of the time, known as thieves' slang.

Either: look back at the examples and explanations of thieves' slang you have collected. Design a glossary of thieves' slang, listed in alphabetical order to accompany the dramascript of *Oliver Twist.*

Or: write a short extra scene for the play in which some of the characters plan or discuss a crime. Use terms of thieves' slang as appropriate.

8 EXPLORING LANGUAGE: THE STYLE OF DICKENS

The playscript has a number of distinct settings: the grim workhouse scenes, the parish undertaker's, the haven of Mr Brownlow's and a number of criminal hideaways. One of the most memorable settings is the ken on Jacob's Island. In the novel, Dickens wrote a full description of this vice-ridden slum:

Near to that part of the Thames on which the church at Rotherhithe abuts, where the buildings on the banks are dirtiest and the vessels on the river blackest with the dust of colliers and the smoke of close-built low-roofed houses, there exists the filthiest, the strangest, the most extraordinary of the many localities that are hidden in London, wholly unknown, even by name, to the great mass of inhabitants.

To reach this place, the visitor has to penetrate through a maze of close, narrow, and muddy streets, thronged by the roughest and poorest of waterside people, and devoted to the traffic they may be supposed to occasion. The cheapest and least delicate provisions are heaped in the shops; the coarsest and commonest articles of wearing apparel dangle at the salesman's door, and stream from house-parapet and windows. Jostling with unemployed labourers of the lowest class, ballast-heavers, coal-whippers, brazen women, ragged children, and the raff and refuse of the river, he makes his way with difficulty along, assailed by offensive sights and smells from the narrow alleys which branch off on the right and left, and deafened by the clash of ponderous waggons that bear great piles of merchandise from the stacks of warehouses that rise from every corner. Arriving at length, in streets remoter and less-frequented than those he has passed, he walks beneath tottering house-fronts projecting over the pavement, dismantled walls that seem to totter as he passes, chimneys half crushed half hesitating to fall, windows guarded by rusty iron bars that time and dirt have almost eaten away, every possible sign of desolation and neglect.

In such a neighbourhood, beyond Dockhead in the Borough of Southwark, stands Jacob's Island, surrounded by a muddy ditch, six or seven feet deep and fifteen or twenty wide when the tide is in, once called Mill Pond, but known in the days of this story as Folly Ditch.

Jacob's Island was a real place in London; in this passage, Dickens sets it with some precision.

In a pair pick out and list all the proper names in the passage. For example: Rotherhithe. Dickens paints a negative picture of this setting by his frequent use of superlative adjectives. In the same pair pick out and list all the superlatives you can find. For example: dirtiest, blackest, filthiest, etc.

	Compound adjectives	Adjectives	Concrete details	Alliteration
E.g.	close-built	close	brazen women	*raff & refuse*

Dickens also uses compound adjectives, ordinary adjectives with negative associations, concrete detail and alliteration in this descriptive passage.
List words and phrases from the passage under the following headings:

9 WRITING: A DESCRIPTION IN THE STYLE OF DICKENS
Write a description of a real place you know well in the style of Dickens. Include proper nouns which give a precise setting, compound adjectives, superlatives, concrete details and alliteration.